A BE BETTER NOW BOOK

LIVE SMARTER NOW

100 Simple Ways to Become INSTANTLY Smarter

Written by JACOB SAGER WEINSTEIN

Illustrated by FABIO SARDO

NEW YORK

For Josh and Lisa, with love

"It no longer makes sense to think of people as born with fixed reserves of potential; instead, potential is an expandable vessel, shaped by the various things we do throughout our lives."

—Anders Ericsson

An imprint of Macmillan Children's Publishing Group, LLC
120 Broadway, New York, NY 10271 • OddDot.com
Odd Dot ® is a registered trademark of Macmillan Publishing Group, LLC

Joyful Books for Curious Minds

WRITER Jacob Sager Weinstein
ILLUSTRATOR Fabio Sardo
DESIGNER Tim Hall and Caitlyn Hunter
EDITOR Justin Krasner
VETTER Kevin T. Jones, PhD

Library of Congress Cataloging-in-Publication Data is available.

ISBN 978-1-250-79507-6

First edition, 2023
Printed in China by Hung Hing Printing

10 9 8 7 6 5 4 3 2 1

CONTENTS

PLAN SMARTER 71

DO SMARTER 95

REASON SMARTER 117

INTRODUCTION

Intelligence is not fixed.

Again and again, when psychologists have investigated human intellectual capacity, they've found an astonishing potential for growth. However you use your brain—however creative or strategic or analytical or organized you are—you can always attain a higher level.

Maybe you think that's just my opinion. Maybe you think it applies only to some kind of fuzzy, anything-goes intelligence. But consider the case of IQ. It isn't the only measure of intelligence, but it's certainly an objective measure of one kind of smarts.

And in 1984, social scientist James Flynn made a remarkable discovery:

For at least as long as IQ tests had existed, people had been getting smarter. For a hundred years, across the entire developing world, IQs went up three points a decade.

To this day, nobody is sure why. Maybe humanity got smarter because we ate better (page 22) or read more (page 20). Whatever the reason, if humanity as a whole can do it, then individual humans can, too. Every one of us can be smarter than we are.

This book has one hundred things you can do right now to do just that.

Some are things to learn (like the basics of probability on page 131). Some are things to do (like exposing yourself to black swans on page 76). Some of them are as easy as opening a window (page 127). Others (like the n-back exercises on page 34) are designed to challenge your brain to the limit. Some of them may surprise you. You've probably never heard of enactment cues (page 105), and you might not know that video games are good for you (page 33).

Even when the general idea is familiar, I hope to teach you something new. You probably know that sleep helps you think more clearly, but do you know what the optimum nap length is for improved reasoning (page 122) versus creative inspiration (page 66)? As varied as they are, all 100 tips have one thing in common: they're designed to help you live your smartest life.

ICONS TO LOOK FOR:

Throughout this book, you'll notice a few recurring logos. Here's what they mean.

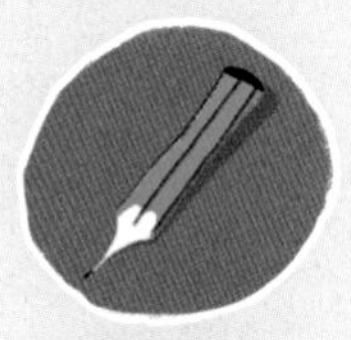

HABITS

Some of the things in this book are one-time lessons to learn. But many of them are habits you can implement, becoming a little smarter each time. If you want help on establishing good habits, see page 96. And if you want a habit tracker, there are some built right into the back of the book jacket.

LEARN MORE

I'm not a neurologist or a psychologist. I'm just a writer who's fascinated by the human brain. In writing this book, I've read and digested the work of a lot of brilliant people who know more than I do. I've done my best to explain their work in a way that gives you concrete steps you can take right away. But inevitably, they've put more ideas in their books than I can present in a one- or two-page exercise. If you want to learn more, the Learn More logo will guide you to brilliant books that go further in depth.

HAPPINESS BONUS

I'm also the author of *Be Happier Now*. It turns out that a number of tips work equally well in either book. The Happiness Bonus logo will draw your attention to techniques that will make you simultaneously happier and smarter.

GROW SMARTER

Grow Smarter is the most general section in this book. Later, we'll dive into specific types of intelligence. For now, we're taking the big-picture, five-hundred-mile-up view. From developing a growth mindset to getting a good night's sleep, this section will help you learn how to help your brain learn.

GROW A GROWTH MINDSET

Growth mindset is the belief that intelligence improves with exercise. **Fixed mindset** is the belief that intelligence is an unchanging trait you're born with.

Unlike fixed mindset, growth mindset encourages you to seek out challenges, which makes you grow. It's the best kind of self-fulfilling prophecy.

STEP 1: Identify a personal limitation. Add *yet* to it . . . but try to be realistic.

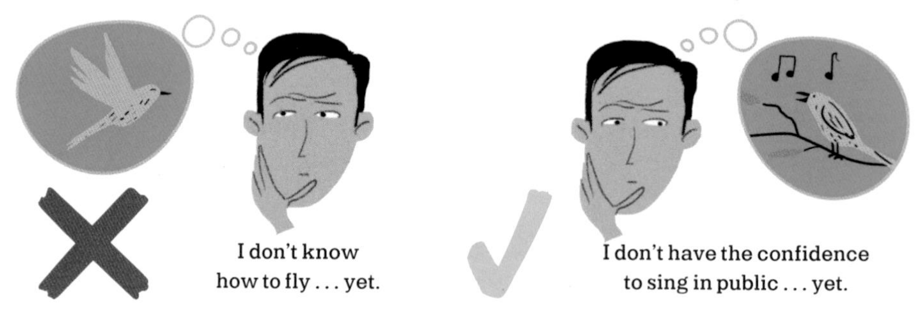

STEP 2: Put yourself in a situation that will stretch you (without physical risk!).

If you want to learn more, read *Mindset: The New Psychology of Success* by Carol Dweck.

☐ If you've given yourself a chance to be challenged (and even fail!), you've succeeded.

ENGAGE IN DELIBERATE PRACTICE

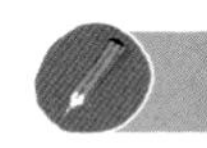

From chess-players to surgeons, top performers master their craft through **deliberate practice**. Whatever skill you want to learn, it can help you achieve mastery.

STEP 1: Identify a stumbling block to mastery, whether it's a tough musical passage or your inability to express your needs in a relationship.

STEP 2: Find an exercise that will mercilessly work that weak point. Play those tricky bars again and again. Express your needs to strangers in the street.

STEP 3: Pay attention to the feedback (including from your own senses). Are you hearing more or fewer wrong notes? Are those strangers nodding sympathetically or edging nervously away? Adjust accordingly.

STEP 4: When you've improved enough that this is no longer your weakest point, go back to Step 1 and identify a new weak point.

If you want to learn more, read *Peak: Secrets from the New Science of Expertise* by Anders Ericsson and Robert Pool.

☐ If you've identified your weakest point and found an exercise to address it, give yourself a win.

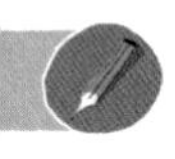

INTERLEAVE IT

The traditional method of practicing a skill is to do it multiple times in a row. This is called **blocking**. If you're an aspiring mad scientist, a practice block might look like this:

Practice evil cackle
Practice evil cackle
Practice evil cackle
Practice evil cackle

A more effective way to learn is **interleaving**, or alternating among different skills:

Practice evil cackle
Practice aiming death ray
Practice intimidating monologue
Practice evil cackle
Practice aiming death ray
Practice intimidating monologue

Because of the constant switching, one session of interleaved practice may give you less confidence than one session of blocking. But in the long run, the extra demands on your brain will help you learn better. Bad news for the meddling superhero trying to stop you!

STEP 1: Engage in deliberate practice (page 3) for a skill.

STEP 2: Practice one or more other skills.

STEP 3: Alternate among skills for your entire practice session.

☐ If you've interleaved two or more skills you want to practice, consider this a triumph.

GET A COACH

If you're a professional athlete, you've already got a full-time professional whose job is to point out areas of improvement. If not, you probably never considered getting a coach. But whatever you do, wouldn't you like to do it at an Olympic level?

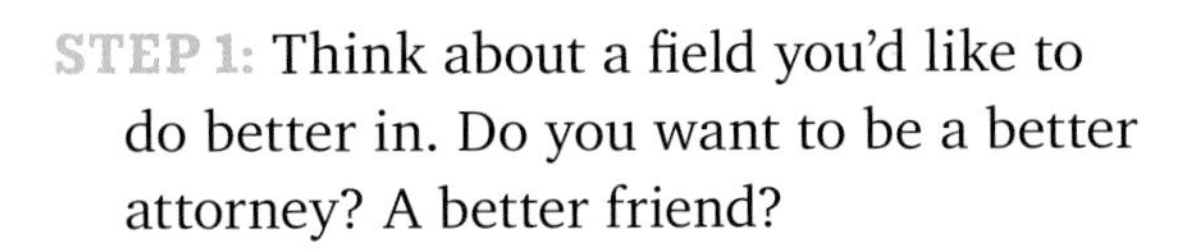

STEP 1: Think about a field you'd like to do better in. Do you want to be a better attorney? A better friend?

STEP 2: Choose somebody whose knowledge of this field you respect.

STEP 3: Ask them for constructive feedback—you want them to spot things you do well and things you can improve.

STEP 4: Let them watch you work. Have them sit in the courtroom while you make your case, or hang out with you and your pals for the day. Pretend they're not there, and encourage them to take notes rather than interrupt you.

STEP 5: Afterward, talk through what you did well and what you can do better.

☐ If you've gotten coaching, or even just reached out to a coach, consider yourself a winner.

GET A GROUP

If you had gone to a pub in Oxford in the 1930s, you might have stumbled on The Inklings, a group of writers that included J. R. R. Tolkien and C. S. Lewis. The Inklings were a **critique group**—a handful of peers who read and commented on one another's work.

Critique groups aren't just for novelists. Whether you're painting portraits or arranging shop windows, getting regular feedback from a group of peers will help you grow.

Unlike a coach (page 5), your critique partners aren't necessarily more experienced than you. Indeed, a critique group often works best when you're all at an equal level. You'll learn together, pulling one another up as you go.

STEP 1: Think about a field you'd like to improve in.

STEP 2: Find a small group of people at roughly your level who are interested in creating roughly the same kinds of things.

Critiquing Constructively

As you review a work, ask yourself:

- What is the creator's goal? Are they trying to make a point, or convey an emotion, or create an experience?
- Where does the work succeed in those goals? Why does it succeed there?
- Where does the work fail to achieve those goals? Why does it fail there? How could it succeed?

STEP 3: Decide on the rules. Will you have a fixed schedule or just swap work when you've got it? Will you focus exclusively on critiques or will you socialize and swap industry gossip? How will you handle members who aren't living up to their responsibilities?

STEP 4: On whatever schedule you've agreed, look over one another's work and offer constructive feedback. See the sidebar for tips.

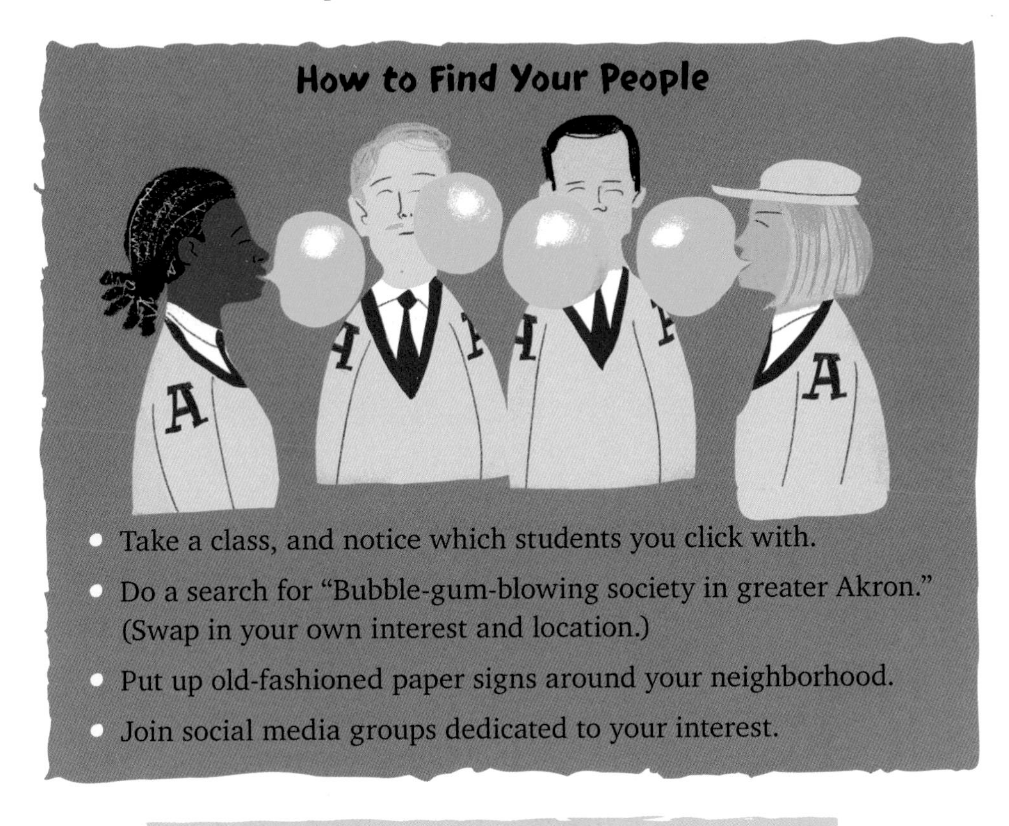

☐ If you've sought out, formed, or worked with a critique group, give yourself the win.

SPACE OUT

If you've ever crammed a fact into your brain by repeating it over and over in a single study session, you've engaged in **massed repetition**. At the end of the session, you had solidly lodged that fact into your short-term memory. Unfortunately, as the name suggests, short-term memory doesn't last. Unless you get something into your long-term memory, it will fade away—and long-term memory is stubbornly resistant to massed repetition.

For long-term learning, you need **spaced repetition**, which involves studying something across multiple study sessions at slowly increasing intervals.

Note that forcing yourself to answer the question, as opposed to just reading the answer, is crucial to studying. Your **hippocampus** is a part of your brain that (among many other things) transfers information to long-term memory, and actively retrieving a fact signals to your hippocampus that it's worth storing.

Spaced repetition is a simple technique, but don't underestimate it. Extensive clinical research over more than a century has shown that spaced repetition is one of the most effective and efficient ways to learn.

In the early days of spaced repetition, students used physical flash cards and an elaborate filing system to track which cards they needed to review when. Nowadays, you can download an app to handle the timing for you.

STEP 1: Search the app store on your preferred system for "spaced repetition." Download one that feels right for you.

STEP 2: Many apps come with an array of premade flash cards. For simple things (like capital cities), you might as well go with premade ones. For more complex or conceptual things, the act of making your own flash cards will help make sure you understand what you're learning.

STEP 3: Practice today's flash cards until the app tells you you're done.

A good spaced-repetition app will notice how often you get questions wrong and show you the hard ones more often, to hammer that tricky knowledge into your head.

DAY 1:	DAY 2:	DAY 3:	DAY 4:
Easy Question Medium Question Hard Question	Hard Question	Easy Question Medium Question Hard Question	

DAY 5:	DAY 6:	DAY 7:	DAY 8:
Hard Question	Medium Question	Easy Question Hard Question	

DAY 9:	DAY 10:	DAY 11:	DAY 12:
Medium Question Hard Question		Easy Question Hard Question	Medium Question

☐ If you've set up a spaced-repetition system, or used one to learn something, give yourself the win.

TAKE A BUS FROM HELSINKI

In 2004, photographer Arno Rafael Minkkinen gave a speech called "The Helsinki Bus Station Theory: Finding Your Own Vision in Photography." Despite the narrow title, Minkkinen's way of looking at growth applies to just about any challenging, long-term pursuit. Word of the Helsinki bus station theory has spread quietly among various creative types, but it deserves to be more widely known.

As Minkkinen pointed out, when a bus starts out in Helsinki city center, there are only a handful of routes it will take. If you don't like heading along a well-trodden path, the solution is to stay on your bus until it gets out of town and paths start to diverge. If you hop off and go back to the central bus depot, you'll never get anywhere.

Suppose, Minkkinen said, you spend years making photographs, only to discover that photographer Sally Mann has done everything you've done, but better. You might be tempted to throw everything you've done out the window and start all over again. If you do that, though, you're hopping off your bus too soon.

FIRST STOP: Same place everybody else is going.

Instead, Minkkinen advised, you should stay on your bus. Keep pursuing the path that interests you, and trust that the longer you do so, the closer you'll get to reaching your own unique destination.

STEP 1: Think about a long-term development goal you've been pursuing.

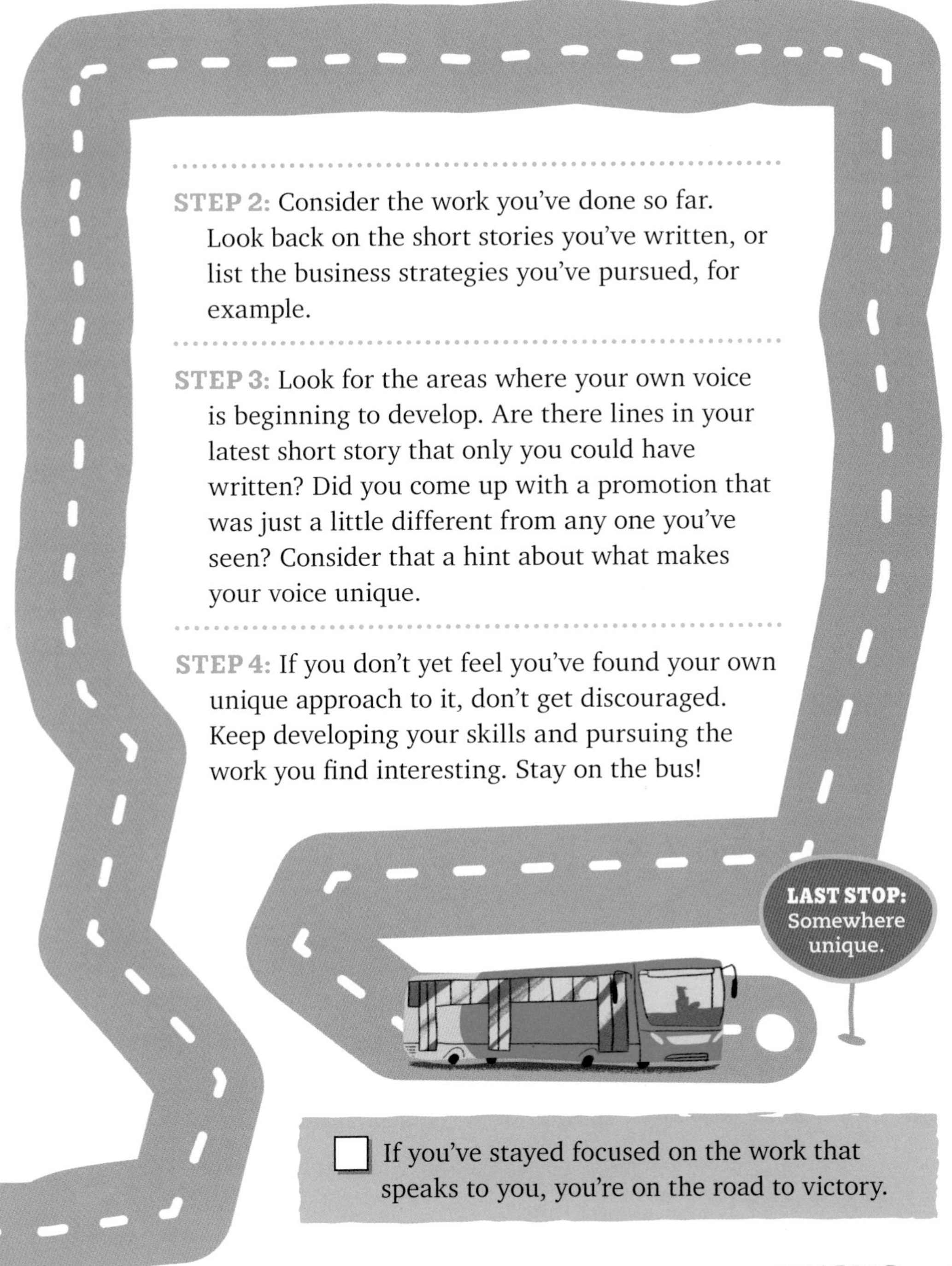

STEP 2: Consider the work you've done so far. Look back on the short stories you've written, or list the business strategies you've pursued, for example.

STEP 3: Look for the areas where your own voice is beginning to develop. Are there lines in your latest short story that only you could have written? Did you come up with a promotion that was just a little different from any one you've seen? Consider that a hint about what makes your voice unique.

STEP 4: If you don't yet feel you've found your own unique approach to it, don't get discouraged. Keep developing your skills and pursuing the work you find interesting. Stay on the bus!

☐ If you've stayed focused on the work that speaks to you, you're on the road to victory.

CHOOSE YOUR VIRTUES

Take a glance out your window. If you see a lightning rod or the United States of America, you're looking at one of Ben Franklin's inventions. Sure, he had a little help on the USA thing, but he accomplished an astonishing amount in his eighty-four years. When he looked back on his life, he credited all his successes to his Plan for Attaining Moral Perfection—a method of self-improvement he invented at age twenty.

STEP 1: Make a list of virtues you think are necessary for a good life. Franklin recommended choosing many specific ones, rather than a few general ones.

The Original Thirteen: Franklin's Virtues

1. **Temperance:** Eat not to dullness; drink not to elevation.
2. **Silence:** Speak not but what may benefit others or yourself; avoid trifling conversation.
3. **Order:** Let all your things have their places; let each part of your business have its time.
4. **Resolution:** Resolve to perform what you ought; perform without fail what you resolve.
5. **Frugality:** Make no expense but to do good to others or yourself; i.e., waste nothing.
6. **Industry:** Lose no time; be always employ'd in something useful; cut off all unnecessary actions.
7. **Sincerity:** Use no hurtful deceit; think innocently and justly; and, if you speak, speak accordingly.
8. **Justice:** Wrong none by doing injuries or omitting the benefits that are your duty.
9. **Moderation:** Avoid extremes; forbear resenting injuries so much as you think they deserve.
10. **Cleanliness:** Tolerate no uncleanliness in body, clothes, or habitation.
11. **Tranquility:** Be not disturbed at trifles, or at accidents common or unavoidable.
12. **Chastity:** Rarely use venery but for health or offspring, never to dullness, weakness, or the injury of your own or another's peace or reputation.
13. **Humility:** Imitate Jesus and Socrates.

STEP 2: Get a way to track your virtues. Franklin did it in a notebook with erasable pages so he could reuse it every year. (Frugality was one of his virtues.) You could also use a spreadsheet on your computer or an app on your phone.

STEP 3: If you're doing it by hand, put your virtues down the side of the chart and the days of the week along the top. At the top of the page, choose one virtue you want to focus on this week.

STEP 4: Try especially hard to live up to the virtue of the week, while keeping an eye on how well you're embodying *all* the virtues. Every evening, look back on your day. For each transgression, make a black mark in the appropriate box. Franklin just tracked his lapses, but if you want some positive encouragement, check off any category you knocked out of the park.

THIS WEEK'S VIRTUE: Kindness

	SU	M	TU	W	TH	F	SA
Efficiency	●			●	✓		
Focus			●	●			
Kindness			✓				
Frugality					●		●
Organization					●		
Honesty						✓	●

STEP 5: At the end of the week, choose a new virtue to focus on.

☐ If you've tracked your virtues, give yourself the win (no matter how many black marks you earned).

HACK YOUR CAVEMAN BRAIN

When your caveman ancestors were evolving their memory, the things they put in it tended to be vivid and dramatic: *Og died after he ate those red berries*, or *When I hear rustling leaves, a tiger is about to pounce*.

Now you need to use that same memory to remember abstract information, like your locker number at the gym or the capital of Germany.

Fortunately, memory masters have developed a vast array of tricks to make abstract things stick in your caveman brain. All you need to do is convert your locker number into something as vivid as a saber-toothed tiger attack. I'll devote the next few pages to these **mnemonic techniques**, but I could fill an entire book with them. Come to think of it, I already did.

If you want to learn more, read *How to Remember Everything: Tips & Tricks to Become a Memory Master* by Jacob Sager Weinstein.

The first tip is to combine two ordinary, forgettable things into one vivid and unforgettable image. It's useful when you need to remember an **association** or link.

Remembering World Capitals

To remember world capitals, come up with a vivid image that combines the country and the capital. If you already have an image for both, it's simple. Otherwise, try using puns and other word associations.

STEP 1: Take the two things you want to link in your memory. Convert each one into something concrete. See above for an example.

STEP 2: Come up with a vivid image that links those two concrete things. Don't just picture them next to each other—imagine them interacting.

STEP 3: Enrich the image with as many different senses as you can. How does it smell, taste, and feel?

STEP 4: When it's time to remember the link, call up the image. It will pop into your mind much more easily than the abstract link would on its own.

☐ If you've used a vivid image to remember a link, picture yourself getting a trophy.

FREE RECALL

A **free-recall exercise** involves pulling newly acquired knowledge out of your brain, which signals to your hippocampus (page 8) that it's worth entrenching in your long-term memory. Plus, it's a handy way of discovering things you didn't absorb the first time.

STEP 1: Very soon after taking a class or reading a book, open up a word processor or pull out a pen and paper. Set a timer for ten minutes.

STEP 2: Write down everything you can remember.

STEP 3: If you run out of memories before you run out of time, keep trying to dredge thoughts out of your brain. Challenge yourself with relevant questions: Who became emperor after Nero? Why shouldn't someone with a nosebleed tilt their head back?

STEP 4: When your ten minutes are up, look at your class notes or reopen the book. See what you forgot to write down, and make a separate note of it.

STEP 5: Next time you study, begin with your notes about what you forgot.

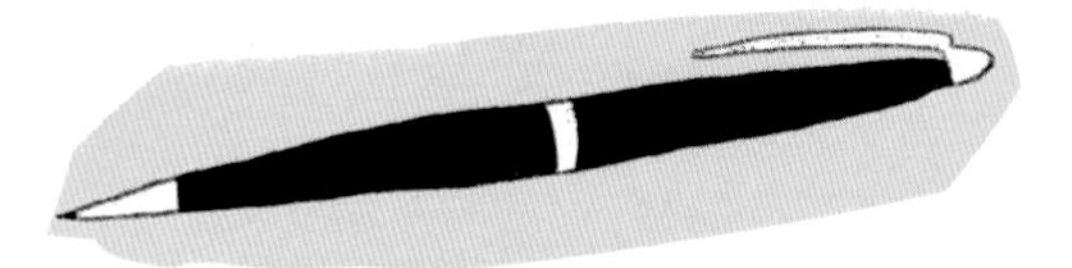

☐ If you've used this free-recall exercise to help you learn, remember this as a victory.

MOVE YOUR MEMORY INTO A PALACE

You never studied the route from your bedroom to your kitchen, but you probably know it by heart. With a technique called the Mind Palace, you can remember any list as easily as the path to your morning coffee.

STEP 1: Think of a list you want to remember, like today's shopping list.

STEP 2: Choose a physical location, real or imaginary, that you know well. Your home works. So does Bikini Bottom.

STEP 3: Pick a starting point, whether that's your bed or SpongeBob's.

STEP 4: Imagine that the first item on your list is at that point. Using all your senses, picture it interacting with something in that space.

STEP 5: Picture yourself strolling to a different room or another location in the same room.

STEP 6: Imagine the next item on the list in this new location.

STEP 7: Repeat Steps 5 and 6 for the whole list.

STEP 8: To recall the list, picture the first location. As you imagine walking around, the vivid images will pop into your mind.

MIND
TROPHY

☐ If you've used a Mind Palace to remember something, put a medal in your Mind Trophy Cabinet.

BUN, SHOE, TREE, DOOR

If you've tried the previous two exercises, you've already gotten some practice at converting abstract things into concrete, easily memorable images. Now it's time for a real challenge: numbers.

To convert numbers into images, just remember a word that rhymes with each digit:

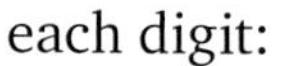

1 = bun **2 = shoe** **3 = tree**

4 = door **5 = hive** **6 = sticks**

7 = heaven **8 = weight** **9 = wine**

STEP 1: Choose a number you want to remember, like the parking space where you left your car.

STEP 2: If it's a short number, you might be able to remember the digits by making them into a story. If you parked in space 435, imagine you drove your car through a *door* and into a *tree*, knocking a *hive* off the branches. The more vividly you imagine these events, the more clearly you'll remember them.

STEP 3: For longer numbers (or if you just can't come up with a story), use a Mind Palace (page 17). Convert each digit into its appropriate rhyming image, and then store each image in the next location.

STEP 4: When you're ready to recall the number, just tell yourself the story or walk through your Mind Palace, recalling each of the individual images.

☐ If you've used number rhymes to remember a number, give yourself one win.

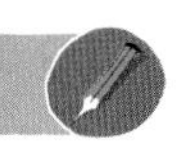

READ ALL ABOUT IT

People who read more fiction score higher on tests of empathy and social skills, and a lifelong habit of reading may help protect you from the effects of a declining memory as you age. If you had a pill that could do all that, and the only side effect was increased risk of library fines, you'd take it every day.

STEP 1: Pick up a book. This one counts. So do graphic novels, romances, children's books, and anything that a snooty gatekeeper ever tried to make you feel guilty about loving. Consistent reading over the course of a lifetime confers the biggest benefits—and you're more likely to be consistent if you enjoy what you're reading.

STEP 2: Read for as long as you enjoy it.

☐ If you've spent fifteen minutes reading, spend a few extra seconds taking the win.

PLAN A READING CHALLENGE

From the previous tip, you know that any reading has real intellectual benefits. But there's some evidence that different kinds of reading benefit you in different ways. Poetic language, for example, seems to increase mental flexibility.

You'll notice I'm using cautious language here, like "seems to" and "some evidence." The studies I'm citing are suggestive, not definitive. Don't force yourself to read a genre you hate if it will turn you off reading completely. But if you're willing to take some intellectual risks, you might just find yourself loving a book you never would have expected.

STEP 1: Make a list of ways to classify books. For example, genre, country of origin, gender or race of author, target age group, or even format.

STEP 2: Within each class, identify a kind of book you don't normally read.

STEP 3: Choose one book in each underread area. Voilà! Your own reading challenge.

☐ If you've planned out a reading challenge or picked up a book from a challenge you already set, give yourself the win.

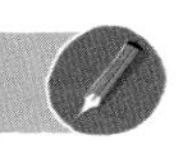

EAT BRAIN FOOD

No matter how much information you cram into your brain, there's a good chance it will slip from your grasp as you age. 5 percent of people in their seventies suffer from dementia. Among people who make it to their nineties, it rises to 37.4 percent.

The good news is, you can take steps now to reduce the risk of it happening to you. Your brain is part of the same complex body as your heart and lungs, and things that are good for them are generally good for your brain, too.

Besides exercise (page 89), that includes a healthy diet. But not just any diet: the MIND diet. Strictly following it is associated with a 53 percent lower chance of getting Alzheimer's. If you aren't up for perfection, even following it "moderately well" is associated with a 35 percent lower risk.

If you're feeling whiplash from ever-changing dietary recommendations, it's worth noting that the MIND diet is essentially a variation on the standard advice to eat more fruits, vegetables, and whole grains, while cutting back on sugar and unhealthy fat. It mainly emphasizes specific fruits and vegetables that seem most associated with healthy brains.

STEP 1: Eat at least some of the foods encouraged by the MIND diet.

STEP 2: Eat less than a tablespoon of butter or margarine a day, and eat less than one serving of red meat, pastry, sweets, and fried or fast food per week.

STEP 3: If you can't stick rigorously to this diet, try at least to eat more of the recommended foods and less of the contraindicated ones.

If you drink, you can include a five-ounce glass of wine per day, but most doctors don't advise starting to drink if you don't already.

The MIND Diet

What to Eat	How Often to Eat It
Fish	Once per week
Berries	Twice per week
Poultry	Twice per week
Nuts and Beans	Every other day
Green leafy vegetables	Every day
Other vegetables	Every day
Olive oil	Every day
Whole grains	Three servings a day

☐ If you've included elements of the MIND diet into your life, feast on your victory.

EAT A LITTLE CHOCOLATE

On page 23, I detailed a wide variety of brain foods. But one is exciting enough that I think it deserves its own page: chocolate, which may improve cognitive skills and memory retention. Not all studies agree on the mental benefits of chocolate. And in the ones that do, the recommended daily amount is pretty small. But in moderation . . . chocolate may be a smart food.

Chocolate also improves mood.

STEP 1: If you've got a kitchen scale, weigh out 1.6 ounces of chocolate. If not, break off about one third of a 3.5-ounce chocolate bar. This is the maximum recommended daily amount of chocolate for health purposes. (The minimum is about 0.35 ounces, if for some bizarre reason, you want wants to eat the minimum amount of chocolate.)

STEP 2: Take a moment to mourn over how small a piece of chocolate this is.

STEP 3: Eat the chocolate.

☐ If you've eaten between 0.35 and 1.6 ounces of chocolate today, give yourself a ton of victory points.

TEACH IT TO LEARN IT

Teachers often say they didn't truly understand a subject until they taught somebody else. Science backs up their intuition. When two Harvard professors tracked student accomplishment for a decade, they found that introducing **peer instruction** resulted in a dramatic leap in test scores. In other words, when students had to teach one another, they learned the subject more deeply and thoroughly.

STEP 1: Pick a subject that you want to master.

STEP 2: Find a friend who wants to learn it, too. Agree on which concepts each of you will be responsible for.

STEP 3: Prepare your first lesson. Learn the key concepts from a book or a video, and think about how to communicate them to somebody else. What are they likely to find confusing? What exercises would help them master key skills?

STEP 4: Meet with your friend. Take turns explaining concepts to each other. As you teach, you may uncover things you don't understand as well as you thought you did. Add them to your homework for the next session.

STEP 5: Pick a time for your next meeting, and repeat the process.

☐ If you've learned something by teaching it to somebody else, consider it a victory.

BE IN THE ROOM WHERE IT HAPPENS

Sometimes when you forget a skill or a fact, it's gone for good. But some memories have a dangling thread, and if you can just tug on it, the whole thing will come flooding back.

Psychologists call this **context-dependent memory**. In plain English, that means the way you store a memory can affect the way you retrieve it. If you walk into your old high school classroom and suddenly remember getting turned down for your prom, you're experiencing context-dependent memory.

Fortunately, context-dependent memory has uses beyond dredging up teenage embarrassments. With forethought, you can use it to prepare yourself for upcoming challenges.

If you've got a presentation coming up, for example, the best place to practice it would be in the room where you'll give it. As you run through it, you're binding the words you'll say (and the confidence with which you'll say them) to the smell of that particular carpet and the hum of that particular air conditioner.

STEP 1: Think about the unalterable circumstances you're training for. Will you be standing up or sitting down? Will it be early in the day or late? Will you be feeling nervous or excited or calm?

STEP 2: Think about the circumstances that will be in your control. What will you wear? Will you have exercised beforehand? What kind of meal will you have eaten, and how long before?

STEP 3: As best as you can, re-create those circumstances while you study or train. Wear the clothes you'll actually wear. Don't forget about your internal state. If you think you'll be nervous, you can even watch a scary scene from a movie to get yourself in the right frame of mind before you practice.

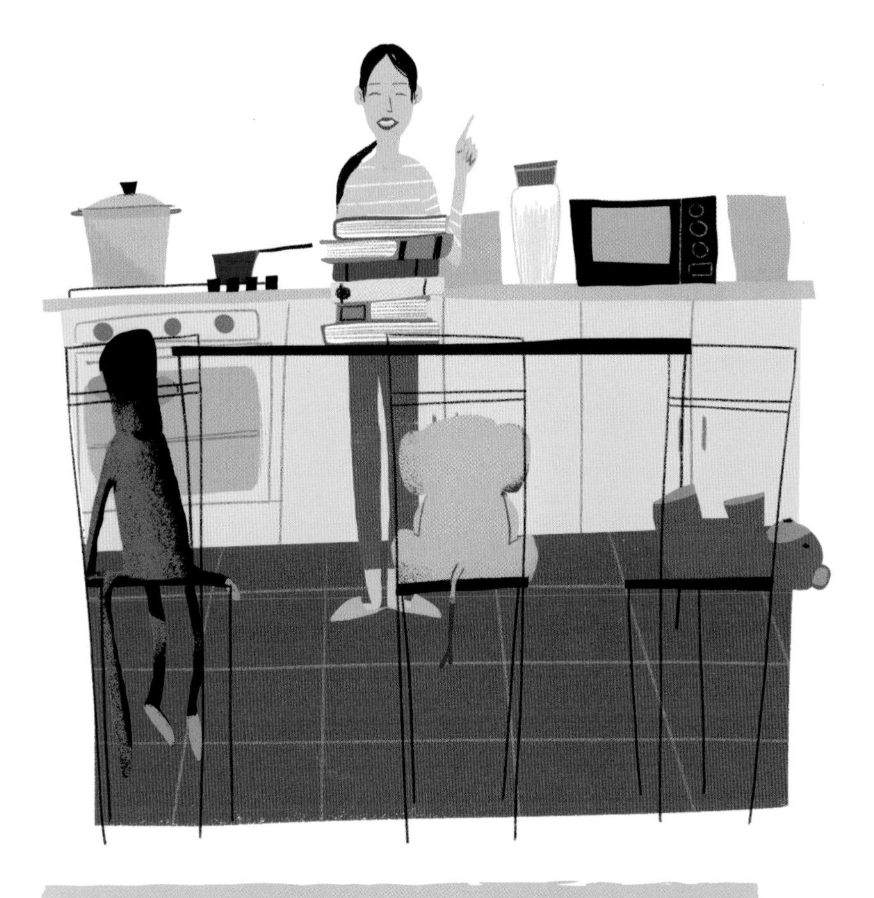

☐ If you've created the right context to prepare for a specific challenge, consider it a victory.

LEARN STUFF BY TRYING TO KNOW STUFF BEFORE YOU LEARN STUFF

You're more likely to remember something that you figure out yourself. Psychologists call this the **generation effect**, and it's very easy to put into practice. To remember the quadratic equation, simply work out the entire history of mathematics from scratch until you discover it independently.

Too much work? Okay, how about this: You can trick your brain into *thinking* it figured it out.

Before somebody teaches you something, try to work it out on your own. When it's finally explained to you, the enhanced *aha!* moment will implant it all the more deeply. As a bonus, the five minutes you spend banging your head against the problem will prepare you to understand the solution faster and more completely.

If you want to learn more about study skills, read *Make It Stick: The Science of Successful Learning* by Peter C. Brown, Henry L. Roediger III, and Mark A. McDaniel.

You can even use this technique to help you remember names at a party. Before somebody introduces themself, guess what name they look like. You're likely to be wrong, but the very act of correcting your wrong guess will implant their real name all the more firmly.

Pretty interesting, don't you think, Linda?

(Hey, it was worth a try.)

STEP 1: Identify a problem you want to solve or a fact you want to learn.

STEP 2: Spend some time trying to work out the answer on your own.

STEP 3: Find out the real answer.

☐ If you've created an artificial *aha!* moment to make a memory stick, consider it a victory.

SLEEP ON IT

If you've used any of the tips in this section, you've put new information and skills into your brain. Now it's time to let your brain **consolidate** what you've learned—to process it and integrate it more deeply with the other stuff you know. While you're at it, you should probably clear out toxins that have built up in your brain during the day.

If that sounds like a difficult and impressive task . . . well, it is. The good news is that your brain accomplishes it while you sleep.

Getting a good night's sleep is one of the most important things you can do for your brain. Besides memory consolidation, a good night's sleep improves your reasoning abilities the next day. Plus, sleep helps protect your long-term brain health.

How to Sleep Smart

- Keep yourself cool. In the winter, set your thermostat for somewhere between sixty and sixty-seven degrees Fahrenheit. In the summer, rather than blast the air-conditioning, it might be cheaper to point a fan at your bed. However you do it, the right bedroom temperature can give you almost twenty minutes of extra sleep over the course of a night.
- Get in and out of bed at roughly the same time every day, even on weekends, and even when you haven't slept well. It takes consistency to program your internal clock.
- Create a consistent pre-bed routine.
- Use your bed only for sleep or things that relax you, like reading. If you answer work emails in bed, your brain will associate bed with work, making it harder to switch off.

STEP 1: Choose the right bedtime. Most people need six to nine hours of sleep per night. If you have to wake up at a certain time in the morning, work backward from there.

Getting enough sleep is one of the single most effective things you can do to make yourself happier.

STEP 2: Sleep well. If that's a challenge, take a look at my tips for happy sleep.

☐ If you got six to nine hours of sleep last night, wake up to victory.

MAKE IT ELABORATE

If I ask you to remember "a, a, c, e, i, m, r," it's unlikely to stick in your head for very long. If I tell you that's the word *America* in alphabetical order, it suddenly becomes much easier.

Although you didn't know it, you've spent your entire life preparing to remember those ordered letters. You learned that the alphabet is a series of letters, that letters form words, and that one of those words is *America*. Remembering "the letters of *America* in alphabetical order" is as easy as hanging a coat on an existing peg. Trying to remember "a, a, c, e, i, m, r" is like trying to make a coat stick to a blank wall.

Combining several hard-to-remember things into one easier-to-remember chunk is called, appropriately, **chunking**. Tying new knowledge to existing knowledge is called **elaboration**. Whether you're memorizing letters or advanced scientific concepts, chunking and elaboration will help it stick.

STEP 1: Think about something you want to remember.

STEP 2: Can you chunk it together into one easier-to-remember unit?

STEP 3: Can you tie it to a fact or concept you already know? Sometimes there will be a natural link. If you're learning about centrifugal force, you can think about how it relates to your favorite carnival Tilt-A-Whirl. But even an arbitrary association will help. In one classic study, a runner was able to remember astonishingly long sequences of numbers by pretending they were race times.

☐ If you've used elaboration to learn something, consider it an elaborate triumph.

SHOOT SOME ALIENS

In the annals of those who have elevated the human intellect, it's time to add some new names: Mario, Luigi, and Lara Croft. That's right: Video games improve your ability to focus, your executive function, and your working memory.

Surprisingly, there's little evidence that most so-called "brain training" games are any better for you than, say, *Fortnite*. In fact, the greatest benefits from video gaming seem to come when you're engaged in what you're playing, so don't force yourself to stick with a boring game just because you think it's good for you. (One possible exception: the n-back test. See page 34 for more on that.)

Of course, as with any pleasurable activity, video games stop being good for you when they start being addictive. So play video games for as long as they're fun. Stop when they become an obligation or a compulsion.

STEP 1: Find a video game you enjoy.

STEP 2: Play it for as long as it's fun.

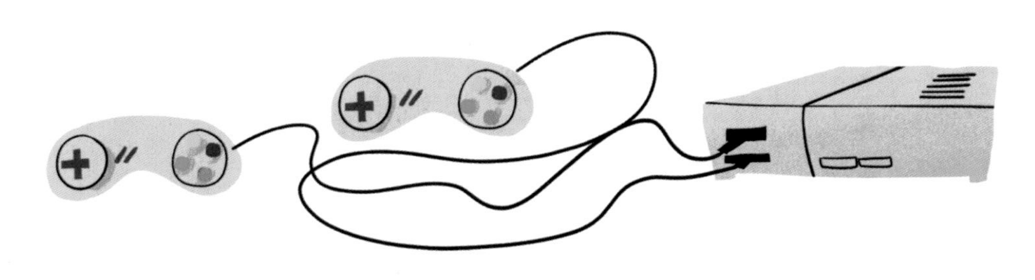

☐ If you've had fun playing one video game today, give yourself the win (even if you got blown up).

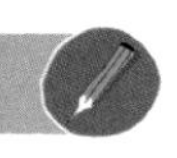

GO N-BACK TO YOUR FUTURE

As I said on page 33, the evidence is mixed for most brain-training games. There's one main exception: **dual n-back exercises**.

Briefly, n-back exercises challenge your **working memory**, which is your ability to hold things in the forefront of your consciousness.

If I go into more detail, I'm going to make things sound more confusing than they really are. Instead, just search your favorite app store for "n-back test," and try one of the apps you find; n-backs are easier to understand when you actually do them.

STEP 1: Search your device's app store for "dual n-back." Or, if you prefer, do a web search for "dual n-back online."

STEP 2: Find an app you like. Most of them are pretty similar, so don't spend too much time looking for the perfect one.

STEP 3: Play the game. Twenty to thirty minutes of practice daily has been linked to improved working memory. It's possible (but not yet proved) that shorter sessions may have benefits as well.

☐ If you've challenged yourself with an n-back test, store a victory in your working memory.

CREATE SMARTER

Create Smarter is about creative intelligence—about using your brain to invent, to dream, and to share your ideas with the world. From learning from your heroes to using your mistakes, this section will expand your creative potential.

COPY YOUR HEROES

When we picture great artists, it tends to be at the peak of their originality. What we often forget are the many years they spent imitating past masters.

Eighty-year-old Picasso was one of a kind—but sixteen-year-old Picasso frequently copied El Greco.

Twenty-year-old Beethoven was so influenced by a certain classical great that he wrote on one of his own scores, "This entire passage has been stolen from Mozart."

Even if you never reach the level of a Picasso or a Beethoven, you can improve your own craft by imitating the work of your creative heroes.

This particular exercise is one of several tips *Live Smarter Now* takes from Ben Franklin. He's the master I imitate when I want to write better self-improvement books.

STEP 1: Think about a creative skill you want to improve. Do you want to get better at choosing colors in a painting? At crafting elegant prose?

STEP 2: Pick a specific work that does this skill masterfully.

STEP 3: Try to figure out the reason behind the creative choices. Why did she arrange the sentence in that particular way? Why did he put that particular green next to that particular purple?

STEP 4: Jot down some notes about the contents of the work, but don't be too detailed. You want just enough to jog your memory.

STEP 5: Put the artwork aside for a day or two.

STEP 6: Try to re-create it from memory. Write the master's original essay, trying to get as close as you possibly can to their original word choice. Paint the master's original portrait, trying to get the colors as close as you can to theirs. You're allowed to use your notes, but don't look at the actual work of art yet.

STEP 7: When you're done, compare your copy with the original. Where did the master make different choices than you? How is their work better? Also notice differences that you're proud of—things that make your work feel more like *your* work. Those are hints to follow as you develop your own voice.

☐ If you've learned from one master, you've triumphed.

CHOOSE QUANTITY OVER QUALITY

A photographer named Jerry Uelsmann did an experiment with his students. He divided them in half and told one group they'd be graded purely on the number of photos they turned in, no matter how good or bad they were. The other group was told they'd be graded on quality; if they turned in a single perfect photograph, they'd get an A for the term.

He wasn't surprised that the quantity group produced more photos. What surprised him was that the quantity group turned in *better* photos. Freed from the pressure of greatness, they took more creative risks. Even the risks that failed taught them lessons they took into the next couple of dozen photos.

It turns out nobody can produce a single perfect photo . . . but anybody can produce a group of one hundred that has some fascinating failures and some amazing successes. As two-time Nobel Prize winner Linus Pauling once said, "The best way to have a good idea is to have lots of ideas."

STEP 1: Choose a creative skill you want to get better at.

STEP 2: Challenge yourself to produce as many different works as you can, without caring about quality.

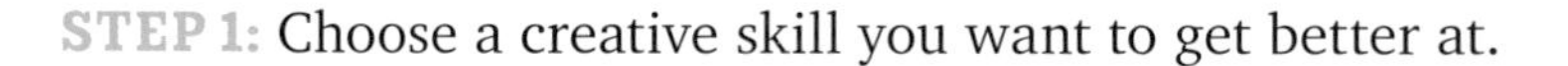

STEP 3: If you stumble onto an interesting technique or subject, feel free to explore it. But other than that, don't judge yourself until you're done.

STEP 4: When you finish, look back. Harvest any works that are successful. Learn what you can from any that aren't.

☐ If you've forgotten about quality and focused purely on quantity, consider that one of many victories.

LET YOUR AUDIENCE MAKE THE CONNECTION

Jaws is at its scariest when we can only see the shark's fin. The *Mona Lisa* would be far less captivating with a caption explaining exactly why she's smiling. As Spielberg and da Vinci both knew, the most effective stories take place inside the audience's mind. Your own storytelling can become more effective with a little bit of careful omission.

STEP 1: Think about any story you want to tell, whether in conversation or on the page.

STEP 2: Find a spot where you're tempted to explain something in detail to your audience. ("So there's this guy I met once, on New Year's Eve, in New York City, just a few moments before midnight.")

STEP 3: Ask yourself: What essential clues does the audience need to figure this out themselves? If this were a movie, how could you set the scene with the fewest images?

STEP 4: Replace your detailed exposition with those essential clues. ("Times Square. The ball is already starting to drop.")

STEP 5: Try out your story on a few sample audience members to test if your clues are clear enough.

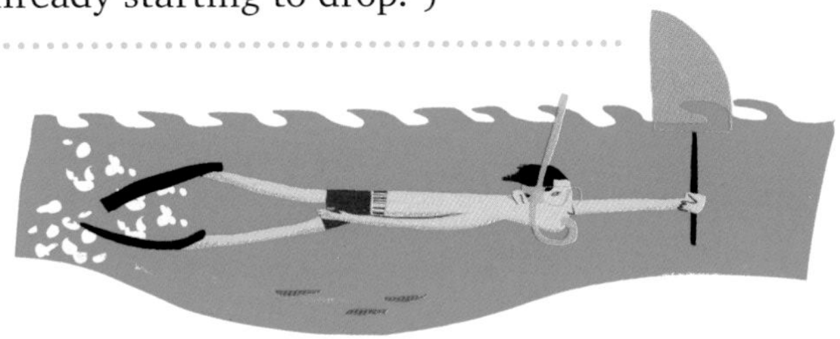

☐ If you've conveyed the same idea in fewer words and more vivid images, give yourself a win.

SEE YOUR WORK THROUGH SOMEBODY ELSE'S EYES

As somebody who has written for both kids and grown-ups, I can tell you: Writing for kids is harder. I have to imagine every sentence from the perspective of somebody in a very different stage of life than mine.

And the people who design amusement parks have to see things from a kid's *literal* perspective. Disney Imagineers even put on kneepads and crawl through the parks to experience a child-height sight line. (Fun Disney World tip: When you pass the Cinderella Fountain in the Magic Kingdom, crouch down until your eyes are at kid-level. Then—and only then—the crown painted on the wall will line up perfectly with Cinderella's head.)

Even when your audience isn't three feet shorter than you, you still need to take their perspective into account. A creative work is meant to be experienced—and your work will be stronger if you can experience it the way your audience will.

STEP 1: Consider a project you're working on, whether it's a pitch for a client or a massive painting for the ceiling of the Sistine Chapel.

STEP 2: Ask yourself: Who are you making this for?

STEP 3: Figure out how your audience will experience things differently than you. Think about physical differences—what angles will they view it from? Is their hearing better or worse than yours? Think about psychological perspective as well. What assumptions do you make that they won't?

STEP 4: Test your work from those new perspectives. Does your fresco still look good when it's partially blocked by tourists' phones? Is the story you're telling coherent for somebody who doesn't know the name of your fourth-grade crush?

STEP 5: You don't have to make your work universally accessible—no work can please everybody. But make sure you repeat this process for everybody in the specific audience you want to reach.

☐ If you've rethought one creative project from the point of view of an audience member, give yourself the win.

BE YOUR OWN SALIVATING DOG

Your brain may feel like a single unit—a *you*—but it's actually a collection of networks. Sometimes when you desperately need to activate the focusing-on-a-project network, the thinking-about-pastry network insists on activating instead.

Fortunately, if you use two parts of your brain together enough, then activating one will automatically activate the other. As scientists say, "Neurons that fire together wire together." This was famously demonstrated by Russian psychologist Ivan Pavlov, who played a specific noise every time he fed his dogs and discovered that they soon came to salivate when they heard the noise, whether or not food was present.

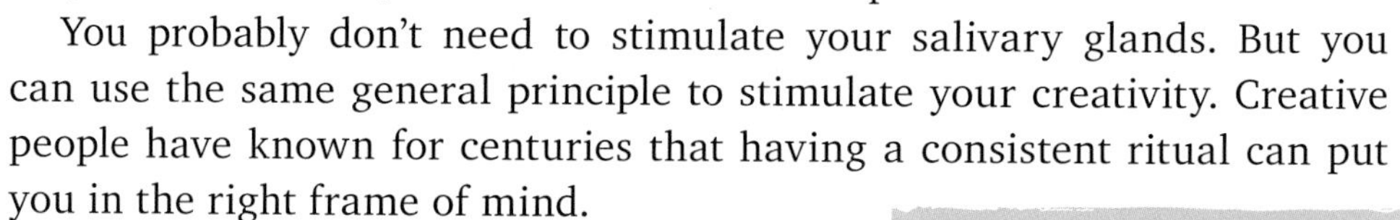

You probably don't need to stimulate your salivary glands. But you can use the same general principle to stimulate your creativity. Creative people have known for centuries that having a consistent ritual can put you in the right frame of mind.

It doesn't matter what that ritual is—what matters is that you're consistent. As novelist Haruki Murakami put it, "The repetition itself becomes the important thing."

To learn more, read *Daily Rituals* by Mason Currey.

Rituals of Creative People

- Beethoven counted exactly sixty beans per cup for his morning coffee.
- When composer Igor Stravinsky was stuck, he'd clear his thoughts by doing a handstand.
- Louis Armstrong had a two-hour-long preshow routine that included drinking honey to "wash out the pipes" and putting a special salve on his lips.
- Edith Wharton would write in bed with her dog under her left arm.

STEP 1: Invent a ritual you can consistently repeat. It can involve any combination of senses—the sound of a certain song or the taste and smell of coffee prepared a certain way.

STEP 2: After you perform your ritual, engage with your creative work.

STEP 3: Even if the work is going badly, stick with it. If you perform your ritual and then let yourself check social media, you're just creating an association with social media. With time, flowing from the ritual into your creative state will become automatic.

Helpful Rituals

Unhelpful Rituals

☐ If you've used a ritual to get yourself in a specific frame of mind, ritually accept the victory.

TAKE A HIKE

Among the rituals that creative people have engaged in, one habit is common enough (and has enough scientific backing) that I want to single it out: taking a walk.

Novelist Richard Wright took his in the morning. Composer George Gershwin took his in the afternoon. Charles Dickens walked alone, while P. G. Wodehouse strolled in the company of four dogs and a neighbor.

They all intuitively understood the link between walking and creativity. That link has now been demonstrated in the lab: In one experiment, 81 percent of participants did better on a test of creativity when they were walking instead of sitting. And the creativity boost continued even after they sat down.

STEP 1: Prepare to record any ideas you have. Bring a pen and paper, a smartphone, or a handheld voice recorder.

STEP 2: Go for a walk. Walking outside gives you an extra creativity boost, but even walking inside on a treadmill helps.

☐ If you've boosted your creativity with a walk, take a victory lap.

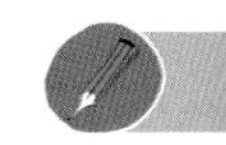

BOOK AN APPOINTMENT WITH THE MUSE

Some writers and artists can't work with a schedule. But some can't work without one.

Toni Morrison and Georgia O'Keeffe both liked to wake up before dawn and watch the sun rise before beginning their creative days.

Rather than wait for the muse to arrive, why not book an appointment with her?

STEP 1: Assign yourself a regular time for your creative work. Depending on your availability, it could be every day or once a month. Set yourself up for success by picking a schedule you can stick with—you can always make it more ambitious later.

STEP 2: Engage with your creative work for the full time you've allotted. Consider starting with a creative ritual (page 42) to get in the right frame of mind.

STEP 3: Don't give up if your session is unproductive. As with creative rituals, creative schedules become more effective the more consistent you are.

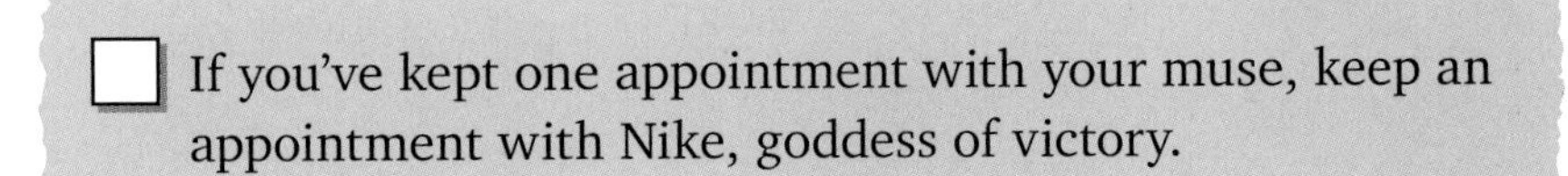

☐ If you've kept one appointment with your muse, keep an appointment with Nike, goddess of victory.

FIGURE OUT THE WRONG ANSWERS

Pixar—the studio that produced *Up*, *The Incredibles*, *Finding Nemo*, *Cars*, and the *Toy Story* movies—has made a science of great storytelling. According to former Pixar artist Emma Coats, one of their principles is this:

"When you're stuck, make a list of what WOULDN'T happen next. Lots of times the material to get you unstuck will show up."

It's great advice—and it applies well beyond making blockbuster animated movies.

STEP 1: Find a problem you're stuck on.

STEP 2: Make a list of solutions that wouldn't work. For each one, explain why, specifically, it wouldn't work.

STEP 3: You may find yourself realizing that one of your impossible solutions actually *would* work. And if not—well, you've been steadily articulating the constraints on your solution, making you that much closer to finding it.

☐ If you've come up with a list of wrong answers for a problem you're facing, you've rightly earned a win.

LET IT INCUBATE

Have you ever returned to a problem that baffled you on a previous day, only to find the answer blindingly obvious? If so, you've experienced **incubation**—the ability of your unconscious mind to keep working on a problem in the background. Incubation is a valuable tool for creative thinking. More important, when my wife comes into my home office and finds me playing a video game, incubation is what lets me claim I'm actually working.

Incubation happens most effectively when you shift your focus to something:

- **Unrelated to the problem you're trying to solve. If you're trying to find exactly the right word for something, don't solve a crossword puzzle to incubate.**
- **Mentally undemanding. Open-heart surgery is *not* a great incubation task.**

Uh-oh. That means doing the dishes is a better incubation task than playing *Assassin's Creed*. If my wife asks, we never had this conversation, okay?

STEP 1: Step away from a problem that's stumping you.

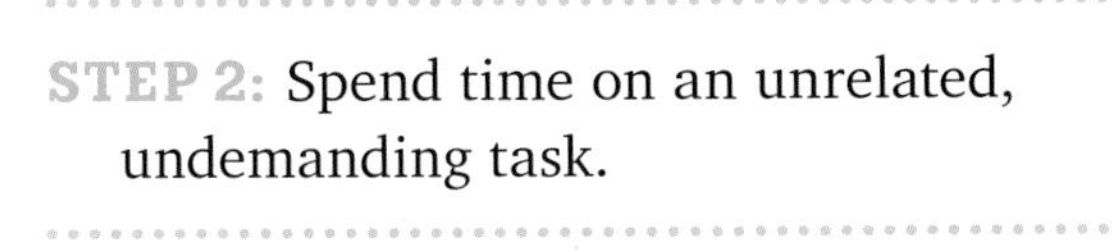

STEP 2: Spend time on an unrelated, undemanding task.

STEP 3: Return to the original problem, and see what your unconscious mind came up with.

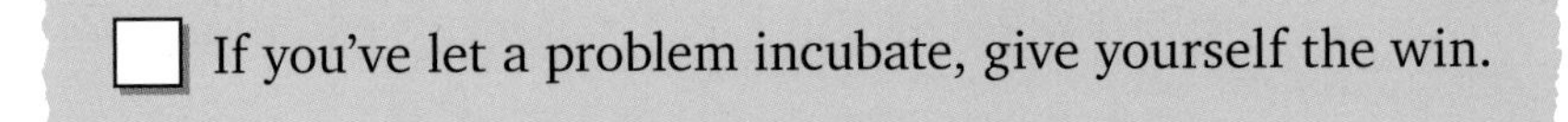

☐ If you've let a problem incubate, give yourself the win.

SWITCH IT UP

Incubation (page 47) is a great strategy when you know you're stuck. Sometimes, though, you can reach a creative dead end without realizing it.

In one small but suggestive study, people were assigned to one of three groups. One group worked on a task and only moved on to another task when it was finished. A second group could switch between tasks whenever they felt stuck. The third group was assigned to switch back and forth at regular intervals, whether they needed to switch or not.

Remarkably, the most creative ideas came from the group that was forced to switch at regular intervals. Even when they didn't know they needed a break, taking one helped them let go of **cognitive fixation**—the tendency to get stuck on a limited set of ideas.

Because this is one small study, I'm not going to suggest you upend your entire way of working. But it's worth experimenting on yourself. You may find that forced task-switching helps you work more creatively.

STEP 1: Find two tasks that require similar types of creative thought—for example, two speeches you're giving on different topics, or a short-term business plan and a long-term business plan. You don't want to pay the cognitive cost of switching between very different tasks—see page 92 for more about that. But keep in mind there will be cognitive costs even with similar tasks. You are trading efficiency for creativity.

STEP 2: Set a timer for ten minutes.

STEP 3: Every ten minutes, force yourself to switch between tasks.

STEP 4: At the end of the session, review how creative you were. Did jumping back and forth help unleash an avalanche of ideas? Or did it just kill your momentum?

STEP 5: If the exercise was successful enough that you choose to repeat it, experiment with the timer length to find the interval that works best for you.

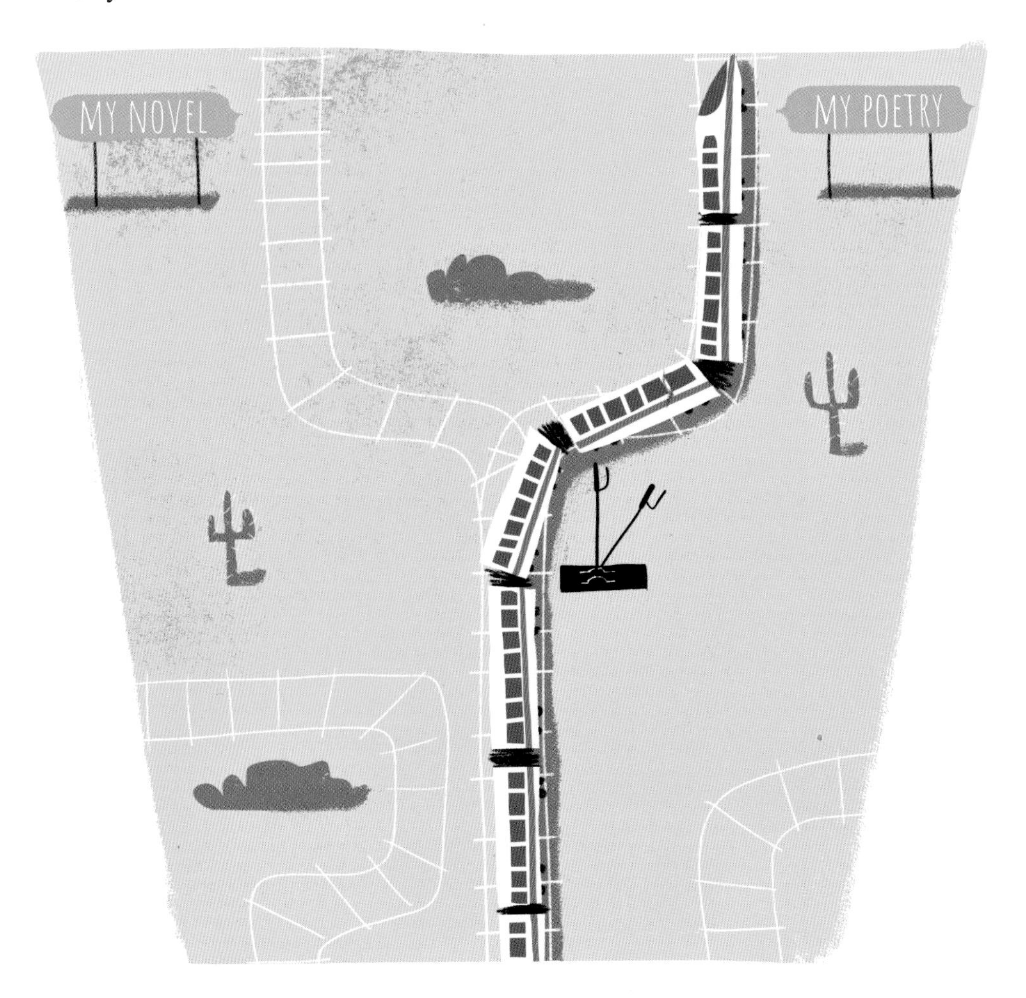

☐ If you've used forced task-switching to generate ideas, switch over to a victory celebration.

WRITE A LETTER TO YOUR MOM

Author John McPhee has a simple solution for writer's block: write a letter to your mother, explaining exactly what your creative problem is and why you can't possibly solve it.

McPhee has written several dozen books, including a couple of bestsellers and one Pulitzer Prize winner. His advice is worth listening to. And if it doesn't work for you—well, you can always write your mom to complain.

STEP 1: Think about a creative problem you're facing, whether it's writer's block or something else.

STEP 2: Choose somebody you can open up to. If you don't have anybody, you can choose John McPhee. Maybe he's not your dad, but he's *somebody's* dad.

STEP 3: Write a letter explaining your problem in detail. Include solutions your recipient might be tempted to suggest, and explain why they won't work.

STEP 4: In the course of explaining the problem and arguing with imaginary solutions, you're likely to stumble on a workable solution. It's up to you whether you send the letter; writing it is the important part.

☐ If you've written one letter explaining a problem you're facing, put in a postscript about your win.

ANALOGIES ARE LIKE KEYS

George de Mestral invented Velcro after noticing a burr clinging to his dog's fur. Ernö Rubik invented the Rubik's Cube after watching water in a river flow around pebbles.

Both inventors were reasoning by analogy. De Mestral used a **near analogy**; the structure of Velcro is directly based on the structure of a burr. Rubik, by contrast, used a **far analogy**; a Rubik's Cube resembles a flowing river only in the most abstract way.

There's some evidence that far analogies can inspire bigger leaps of imagination than near analogies, but experiment to see which kinds of analogies work best for you.

STEP 1: Consider a problem for which you're trying to find a creative solution.

STEP 2: Start with near analogies. How have people in your field solved similar problems? Can you adapt their solution to your situation?

STEP 3: Move your analogies a little further. How have people in different fields (or Mother Nature) solved similar problems?

STEP 4: If you still don't have a solution, take a walk, or flip through a random book. Ask yourself, "How is this like my problem?" for everything you see.

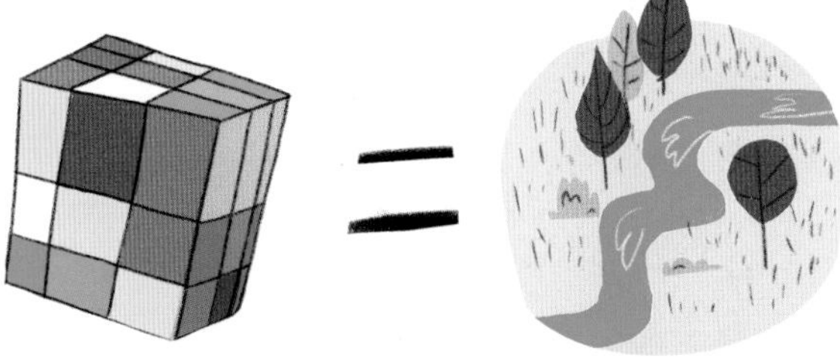

☐ Using an analogy to stimulate creative thought is a lot like winning.

FOLLOW YOUR CURIOSITY

During a particularly low period, scientist Richard Feynman gave up on accomplishing anything. "I'm going to play with physics whenever I want to," he said, "without worrying about any importance whatsoever."

Soon after, in a cafeteria, Feynman saw somebody throw a plate into the air. "I had nothing to do," Feynman said, "so I started to figure out the motion of the rotating plate." Working out the motion of a rotating plate led Feynman to working out the motion of subatomic particles—and to a Nobel Prize.

Following your own curiosity might not lead you to unravel the secrets of the universe—but it can lead you to amazing places.

STEP 1: Notice something that fascinates you, no matter how frivolous it seems.

STEP 2: Follow your curiosity. Dive into the details of how the object of your fascination works, or use it as a springboard for your own crazy ideas.

STEP 3: If your journey bears practical benefits, great. But if not, the time wasn't wasted. You've broadened your mind.

☐ If you've chased your curiosity down one intriguing avenue, you've followed it to victory.

DISTRACT YOURSELF

If you work better in a coffee shop than a library, science has your back. Research shows that people may be more creative with a moderate level of background noise.

Moderate noise can cause **processing disfluency**—it makes your brain work harder, keeping it from easy, everyday modes of thinking. Of course, when there's too much distraction, your brain can't fall into *any* mode of thinking. For many of us, the ideal balance is the gentle hum of voices mixed with the smell of lattes.

STEP 1: Find a moderately noisy environment to work in. If coffee shops aren't for you, play background music or open a window to let in some outside sounds.

STEP 2: At the end of your session, think about whether the noise was the right level. Was your thinking better or worse than usual? Adjust accordingly. (One tip: The older you get, the harder it becomes to filter out distractions. The right noise level for Current You may not be the same as for Past You.)

☐ If you've used moderate background noise to help you be more creative, consider it a triumph.

LAUGH IT UP, BUDDY

You don't need me to make the case for happiness. It's an inherent good. But as an added bonus, **positive aspect** (psychologist-speak for "being in a good mood") has been shown across numerous studies to make you a more open-minded and creative thinker.

Sometimes being smarter requires discipline and hard work. Sometimes you just have to let yourself feel good.

STEP 1: Before any project that requires creative thought, put yourself in a good mood. Watch a short, funny video clip, or remember something nice that somebody said to you. (But avoid **goal-directed** good moods. Don't think about a delightful meal you want to bake later, for example.)

☐ If you've deliberately put yourself in a good mood to enhance creative thought, cheer yourself further with thoughts of your win.

BORE YOURSELF INTO INSPIRATION

Author Neil Gaiman has a suggestion for people who want to be more creative: Get bored. As he explains, ideas "come from daydreaming, from drifting, that moment when you're just sitting there . . . To people who say, 'I want to be a writer,' I say, 'great, get bored.'"

Science backs Gaiman up. When your mind isn't being entertained, it's more likely to wander—and to stumble onto original thoughts. Just as incubation (page 47) can help you solve specific problems, boring yourself into a daydream can provide general inspiration.

STEP 1: Put yourself in a good mood (see previous page). Then read a boring book, or wander through a particularly dull neighborhood.

STEP 2: Choose in advance how long you'll subject yourself to boredom, and resist the urge to pull out your phone or otherwise entertain yourself until it's done. You can let yourself write down any ideas that occur to you, but otherwise, just marinate in the boredom.

☐ If you've let yourself be bored, give yourself—*yawn!*—another win.

VOMIT YOUR WAY TO GENIUS

The same principle of forgetting about quality when creating lots of work (page 38) applies to the first draft of any individual work.

As author Barbara Kingsolver said, the first two steps for writing a novel are:

STEP 1: Give yourself permission to write a bad book.

STEP 2: Revise it until it's not a bad book.

As a way of lowering their own expectations, and to emphasize how quickly they should get it out, writers sometimes call their first draft a "vomit draft."

Entrepreneurs have a slightly more decorous term: **minimum viable product**. Getting an MVP out the door lets you quickly learn what your customers really want, allowing you to come up with a more polished version in future steps.

You can't revise a blank piece of paper. You can't fix a product that doesn't exist.

Whatever you're creating, and whatever you label your first version, moving too fast for your self-doubt to catch up can jump-start your creative process.

STEP 1: Choose a creative project.

STEP 2: Pump out a version. Focus on speed and forget about quality.

STEP 3: Put your draft aside for a little while, and recover from your sustained creative effort.

STEP 4: For the first time, cast a critical eye on your own work. What works? What doesn't? What did you discover about the work in the process of creating or reviewing it?

STEP 5: Improve your work as much as you can on your own.

STEP 6: Get feedback. Let some trusted friends read your sonnet cycle, or let a few customers try your product.

STEP 7: Fix any flaws your feedback has uncovered.

☐ If you've pumped out a quick first draft of something, give yourself a quick win.

TAKE THE LONG WAY HOME

Creative people come in all flavors, from the sloppy, paint-covered artist to the inventor who machines their gadgets down to the millimeter. But psychologists have found one trait that consistently correlates with creativity: **openness to experience**.

Broadly speaking, openness to experience measures how willing and able you are to let stuff into your consciousness. This includes stuff from outside your head, like a change in your environment. And it includes stuff *inside* your head, like multiple emotions at once. If the first orange leaf of autumn swells your heart with joy and sadness simultaneously, you probably have a high openness to experience.

It's no surprise that this trait is linked to creativity—which is, after all, the act of taking in the world and your feelings about it and then synthesizing your experiences into something new.

Fortunately, the evidence suggests that it's possible to increase your openness to experience—and, in doing so, your capacity for creativity. The key seems to be exposing yourself to experiences that are both *new* and *cognitively stimulating*.

STEP 1: Think about some mentally challenging thing you don't usually do. Cultural activities are great for this. Just make sure to challenge yourself in some new way. If you're a die-hard opera buff, attend an open-mic night for folk singers instead. Go to a museum you've never visited, or check out that one wing at your favorite museum that you usually skip.

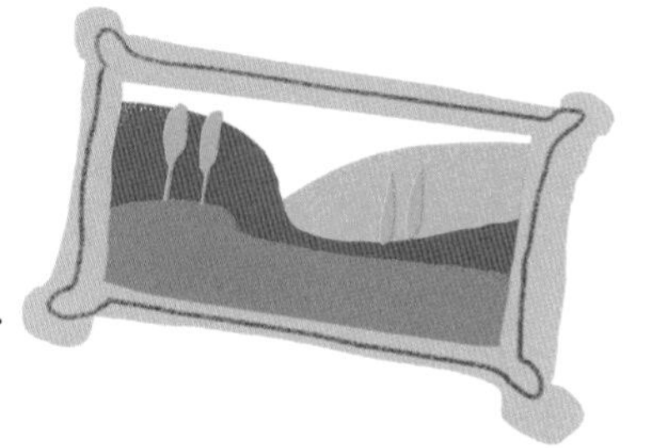

STEP 2: Engage as openly and as actively as you can. Don't just let your mind wander as the concert fades into the background—follow the music, even if doing so doesn't come naturally.

STEP 3: Don't just save challenging experiences for special occasions. Look for opportunities to make mentally stimulating changes in your daily life. Take a new route home from work and actively look for ways the new street you're heading down differs from the one you usually take.

☐ If you've put yourself in one new, cognitively stimulating situation, that's a victory.

REACH FOR THE BLUE SKY

Rational thought and sober-minded analysis have their place in the creative process—but before you can judge your ideas, you need ideas to judge.

Starting in the 1940s, advertising executive Alex Osborne began experimenting with brainstorming, coming up with a series of guidelines that are still useful today.

STEP 1: Restate a problem you're facing as an open-ended question. How can we fix the backlog in our shipping department? How can I persuade my kids to stop fighting?

STEP 2: Do any research you need to. The more information you have about the problem, the more ideas you'll generate to solve it.

STEP 3: Give yourself an objectively measurable goal, like "I'm going to come up with ten ideas in the next ten minutes." Make sure you're measuring quantity, not quality. For now, it doesn't matter if those ten ideas are any good.

STEP 4: Write down every answer that occurs to you. If you're brainstorming with a group, write things down on a whiteboard or some other place where everybody can see it.

STEP 5: If you like an idea, feel free to build on it. And if you don't like it, rather than shooting it down, come up with a new idea you like more.

STEP 6: Of course, if an idea is morally offensive, you don't have to write it down, but don't make any other judgments. Those will come later (page 69). For now, actively encourage outrageous ideas. If you're stuck in a sensible, practical rut, ask yourself some crazy questions. How would you solve this problem if you had an infinite amount of money?

How would you solve it if you weren't afraid to fail? How would Godzilla solve it? For a quick supply of ready-made questions, see the SCAMPER technique (page 62).

STEP 7: Don't give up too soon. Ideas generated late in a session are often the most innovative.

STEP 8: If your brainstorming session points you toward an answer, great! If not, you've still made progress. To paraphrase Thomas Edison, the first step in inventing a light bulb is finding a thousand things that *aren't* a light bulb.

☐ If you've brainstormed freely, think of a new way to describe your win. (Smash hit? Success? Achievement?)

S.C.A.M.P.E.R. AWAY

You can't always brainstorm (page 60) on command. Sometimes you need help coming up with questions that will provoke offbeat and creative answers. For these situations, creativity expert Bob Eberle developed the SCAMPER technique. It stands for:

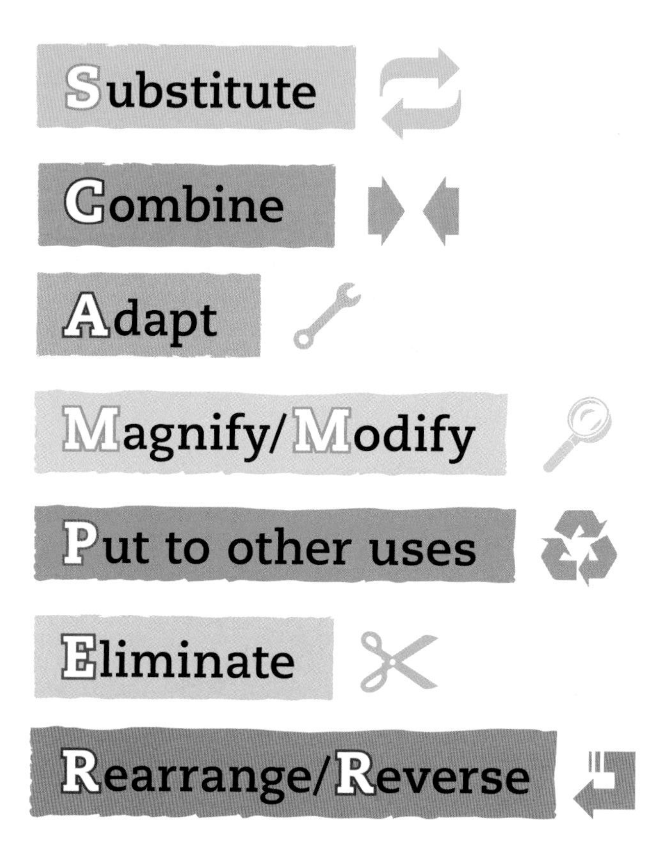

When you're blocked, try running through the steps of SCAMPER and see what comes skipping out of your imagination.

STEP 1: **Substitute.** Take an existing idea, and change one or more elements to something else. Make your mom's chocolate chip cookie recipe—but with potato chips.

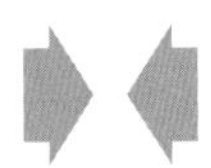

STEP 2: **Combine.** Take two preexisting ideas and mash them together into something new.

STEP 3: **Adapt.** Adjust an existing product or idea to work better.

STEP 4: **Magnify/Modify.** Distort an existing idea. Make some aspect of it bigger or smaller.

STEP 5: **Put to other uses.** A classic real-life example is the Microplane grater, which started as a woodworking tool before finding success as a food grater (and, eventually, a skin exfoliator).

STEP 6: **Eliminate.** Can you remove parts of an existing idea? Can you streamline a process?

STEP 7: **Rearrange/Reverse.** What if you put the last chapter at the beginning of the story? What if the fingerprint reader went under the screen?

☐ If you've used the SCAMPER technique to come up with creative answers, scamper over to the check box.

FOLLOW YOUR DREAMS

Sleep doesn't just help you retain things you've already learned (page 30). A good night's sleep makes you more creative when you wake up.

Sometimes you can even solve problems while dreaming. Paul McCartney came up with the melody to "Yesterday" in a dream. His sleeping mind hadn't come up with lyrics, so he put in dummy lyrics the next morning: "Scrambled eggs/ Oh my baby how I love your legs/ Not as much as I love scrambled eggs." (Maybe he should have slept a little longer.)

You can prime your subconscious to work on a specific problem. One study found that smelling a scent while trying to solve a puzzle, then diffusing it in your bedroom while you sleep, made you more likely to figure out the solution while you dozed.

STEP 1: Choose a problem you want to solve. Dreams are particularly helpful with problems that require vivid visualization or out-of-the-box thinking.

STEP 2: Create an association between your sleep environment and your creative task. Wear your pajamas while you're working on your novel. Or use the same scented air freshener in your painting studio and your bedroom.

STEP 3: If it's a relaxing problem, you can think about it shortly before you go to sleep. If it's more likely to disturb your rest, build plenty of time to unwind.

STEP 4: Keep pen and paper by your bed. Sleep time inspiration can fade quickly.

☐ If you've slept on a problem, wake up to a win.

USE LOW-ENERGY TIMES FOR CREATIVE THOUGHT

A well-rested mind is better at filtering out irrational thoughts. But sometimes that filter can get in your way. One study found that people are most creative at the time of day when they (and, therefore, their critical minds) are least alert.

STEP 1: Pay attention to your energy level throughout the day. When are you drowsiest or most fatigued? For many people, this will be around 3 PM.

STEP 2: If you have control over your schedule, plan to do rational work that requires clear focus during your alert times.

STEP 3: Use your drowsy period for brainstorming and other creative tasks.

☐ If you've taken advantage of a drowsy time to access your creativity, consider it a triumph.

MICRONAP TO MAJOR INSPIRATION

Elsewhere, I discuss the mental benefits of a full night's sleep (page 30) and a short nap (page 122). Those are extensively studied phenomena, with plenty of scientific backing.

I now want to delve into a quirkier technique, beloved by certain creative people, but relatively unstudied by scientists: the **micronap.**

The micronap gets its potency from the **hypnogogic state**—the moment right between waking and sleeping. Salvador Dalí, Thomas Edison, and Edgar Allan Poe all used micronaps to generate ideas.

STEP 1: Sit in a comfortable chair, holding something in one hand. It should be heavy enough to make a noise when it hits the floor, but not too heavy to hold. Edison used a metal ball; Dalí used an iron key.

STEP 2: If you're trying to solve a specific problem, hold it in your mind for a moment. Close your eyes, and let yourself drift off to sleep.

STEP 3: When you enter a hypnogogic state, you'll naturally relax your grip, and the object will crash to the floor, waking you.

Dalí's alarm clock.

☐ If you've taken one micronap, give yourself a macro-win.

WRITE MORNING PAGES

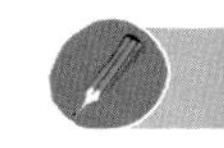

In *The Artist's Way*, her influential book on creativity, Julia Cameron recommends beginning your day with a simple technique called "morning pages." Author Anne Lamott has described the process as "kind of a cognitive centering device, like scribbly meditation."

STEP 1: Before bed, put paper and pen somewhere easily accessible.

STEP 2: As soon as you wake up, fill up three pages with stream-of-consciousness writing. Don't worry about punctuation or spelling or even content. Just write down your thoughts. If you feel like an idiot writing down your thoughts, you can write, "I feel like an idiot."

STEP 3: Don't stop writing until you've filled up three pages with words.

STEP 4: If you happen to have come up with a useful idea while writing them, you're allowed to make a note of it, but otherwise, just put the pages aside and get on with your day. They're purely a brain-loosening creative exercise; they don't need to have any tangible outcome other than a clearer head.

☐ If you've started the day with morning pages, end it in triumph.

CONSTRAIN YOURSELF

An author named Theodor Geisel once made a bet with publisher Bennett Cerf. If Geisel could write a children's book using only fifty distinct words, he'd win fifty dollars. Geisel succeeded, and when the book was published under his pen name, Dr. Seuss, *Green Eggs and Ham* became a runaway bestseller.

It's not just children's books that benefit from constraints. Serious grown-up composer Igor Stravinsky once said, "The more constraints one imposes, the more one frees one's self."

STEP 1: Take any creative project you want to enhance.

STEP 2: Put some constraints on it. How would you write it if you couldn't use the letter *e*? How would you build it if you could only use cardboard?

STEP 3: Try your hardest to make it work within those constraints.

STEP 4: If you simply can't make it work within the constraints, take a step back. What have you learned about the requirements of your project? Can you now make it better without the constraints?

☐ If you've enhanced a creative project by adding constraints, it's an unconstrained victory.

CONVERGE ON THE ANSWER

Generating ideas is just the beginning of the creative process. Once you've got those ideas, you've got to figure out which ones to run with, and that means narrowing your focus. Experts on creativity call this **convergent thinking**, and they've generated some rules for doing it effectively.

STEP 1: Review your ideas when you've got the time to be thoughtful. You've put in the effort to generate these ideas; make sure you can give them a fair hearing.

STEP 2: Start with the positive. For each idea, consider what's good about it.

STEP 3: Now it's time to let your inner critic reengage. Check each idea against your objectives. Does it move you closer to your goal?

STEP 4: Be alert to opportunities for improvement. Is there a way to keep an idea's strengths while fixing its weaknesses?

STEP 5: If an idea doesn't bring you closer to your goals and can't be fixed, get rid of it without mercy.

☐ If you've narrowed down a list of brainstormed ideas, consider it a triumph.

TREAT MISTAKES AS GIFTS

Improv comedians have a saying: "Treat mistakes as gifts." If your scene is supposed to be set in a barn, and you accidentally refer to it as a library—well, congratulations! Your library is now inside a barn, which is vastly more interesting.

Even if you're not doing improv, your mistakes can be a rich source of creative inspiration. Treat them as gifts, and they may turn out to be just that.

Useful Mistakes Throughout History

- **In 1903**, chemist Édouard Bénédictus knocked a glass flask onto the floor. It broke—but the shards stuck safely together. Bénédictus realized that the flask had previously held a liquid plastic called cellulose nitrate, and the residue was enough to hold the pieces together. Bénédictus had just invented safety glass.
- **In 1970**, Spencer Silver, a scientist at 3M, failed at inventing a strong adhesive and ended up with a particularly weak one. Years later, his colleague Arthur Fry realized that weak glue was perfect for making things temporarily stick together. Together, Silver and Fry had invented the Post-it Note.

STEP 1: Think of a creative mistake you've made—a plot hole in a story you're working on, or an idea that didn't turn out the way you wanted, or some project that went awry.

STEP 2: Reframe the mistake as a gift. What benefits does it have? Although it might have been a failure for your original goal, is it a success at a different goal?

☐ If you've managed to view one mistake as a gift, give yourself the win.

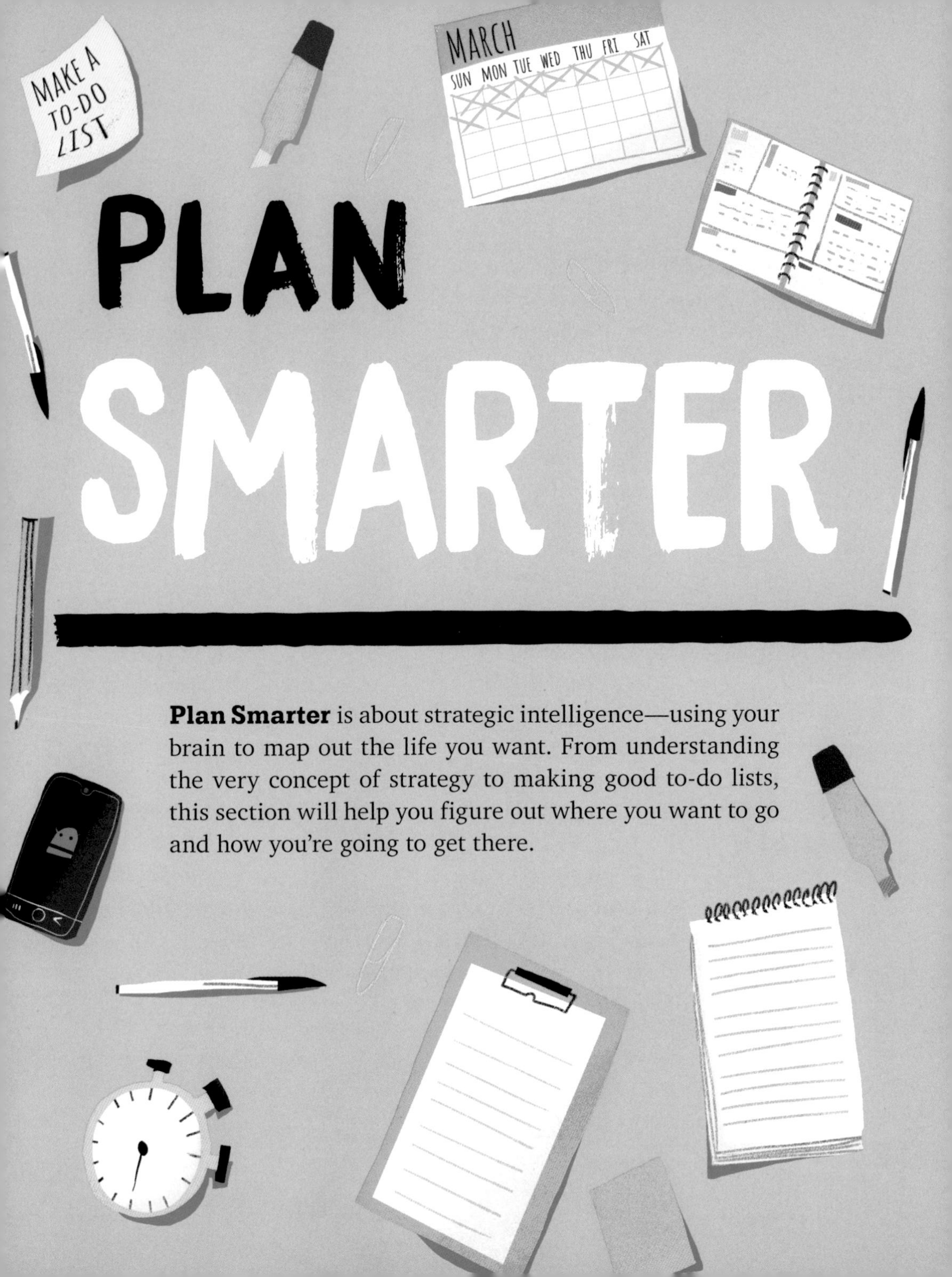

PLAN SMARTER

Plan Smarter is about strategic intelligence—using your brain to map out the life you want. From understanding the very concept of strategy to making good to-do lists, this section will help you figure out where you want to go and how you're going to get there.

START WITH STRATEGY

Knowing the difference between strategy and tactics can help you apply both more effectively.

Tactics are what you use to win a battle. **Strategy** is what you use to decide which battles are worth fighting. Kidnapping your boss's Chihuahua is an effective tactic to make him give you a day off—but a poor strategy for keeping your job.

Planning should always begin with strategy. There's no point in winning a battle if you don't know what you're fighting for.

STEP 1: Think about something you want to achieve in life.

STEP 2: Consider the overarching milestones you plan to reach on the way. This is your strategy.

STEP 3: Work out the expendable resources you'll need to reach those milestones. In a literal battle, it would be troops and ammunition. In your life, it might be time, or money, or social capital.

STEP 4: Figure out the steps you'll have to take to reach each milestone. This is your tactical plan. Make sure no step uses up resources you'll need later.

STEP 5: Some milestones may be too far in the future, or too dependent on circumstances, to work out a concrete tactical plan. Don't get hung up on them. Preserve the resources that Future You will need, and trust yourself to work it out when you get there.

☐ If you've distinguished between strategy and tactics in making plans, distinguish between victory (you!) and loss (not you!).

PERFORM A PREMORTEM

Everybody knows that hindsight is twenty-twenty. Looking back on the past is always easier than predicting the future.

Remarkably, even before an event happens, *imagining* you're looking back on it can make you more realistic about the likely outcome, preventing overconfidence and helping you plan for setbacks. This technique is called **prospective hindsight**—or, more colloquially, a **premortem**. One study found it can make you 30 percent more detailed in your predictions.

STEP 1: Imagine it's the future and you've just gotten bad news: Your current project failed utterly. Your plans ended disastrously.

STEP 2: Now imagine you're performing a postmortem on this failure. What went wrong? If it's a solo project, write down as many likely reasons for failure as you can. If it's a group project, get your colleagues to do the same.

STEP 3: Back in the real-world present day, look at each possible reason for failure and ask yourself: What can I do to prevent this from happening?

☐ If you've planned for at least one likely source of failure you didn't see before, give yourself a win.

IMAGINE YOU'RE YESTERDAY-YOU

It can be surprisingly hard to empathize with your own emotions. When you're full, you forget how intense hunger can be. When you're away from your phone, you forget just how tempting social media is. Psychologists call this the **cold-to-hot empathy gap**.

It has pernicious consequences: When we're making plans, we underestimate the pull of temptation and overestimate our self-control. This is called **restraint bias**.

Just knowing it exists can help you plan around it. Plus, putting yourself in a specific frame of mind can help you predict how you'll react when you're in the same state.

VS

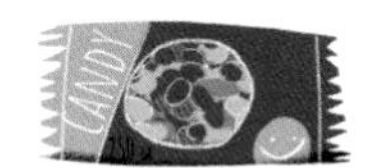

STEP 1: Notice when your plans depend on self-control. Are you buying an economy-size tub of M&M's because *this* time you won't eat it all in a day?

STEP 2: Assume that you will display exactly as much self-control in the future as you have in the past. How will that interfere with your goals?

STEP 3: Revise your plan to counteract temptation. Even if it's not as cost-effective, should you buy a much smaller bag of M&M's?

STEP 4: Put yourself in the appropriate state and see if your plan still make sense. Does your estimate of future candy consumption change once your stomach starts growling?

☐ If you've accounted for the level of self-control you have (rather than the level you want to have), you've triumphed.

IMAGINE YOU'RE SOMEBODY ELSE ENTIRELY

You know those logical fallacies that other people fall into—those weird mental lapses that you are completely free from?

Well, I've got some bad news:

Not believing you're subject to the same mental lapses as everybody else is one of the mental lapses you're subject to. That's why you should always check your plans by asking yourself: How would this go if one of those other bozos tried it?

STEP 1: Consider a plan you're making for yourself—starting an entirely pineapple-themed café, for example.

STEP 2: Imagine some other average person is the one carrying it out.

STEP 3: What mistakes would that average person make? Would they foolishly assume that everybody loves *their* favorite fruit, when you know that *your* favorite fruit is objectively better?

STEP 4: Adjust your plans to account for the slim possibility that you'll make the same mistakes other people would. Test your product, juuuuuust in case the world isn't ready for pineapple coffee with pineapple foam.

☐ If you've rethought your plans in light of an average person's mistakes, did you consider it a win? The average person would.

LOOK FOR BLACK SWANS

Philosopher Karl Popper once said, "No number of sightings of white swans can prove the theory that all swans are white. The sighting of just one black one may disprove it."

From that quote, investor and author Nassim Taleb developed the idea of the **black swan**—the unexpected event with significant consequences.

With a **negative black swan**, the positive consequences are limited, but the negative are effectively infinite. If you drive at twice the speed limit, the best outcome is that you get home a little early. The worst is that you crash into a passing oil tanker and die.

With a **positive black swan**, it's the other way around. The most I can lose from writing this book is the time I spend on it. If it becomes a bestseller, my upside is infinite.

To learn more, read *The Black Swan* by Nassim Taleb.

While any individual black swan is unlikely, life is long enough that you'll eventually encounter *some* black swans. By definition, you can't predict a specific black swan, but you can reduce your exposure to negative ones and increase your exposure to positive ones.

If you own insurance, you're already doing this. Any specific sequence of events that results in your house burning down or your spouse dying young is pretty unlikely. But there are enough ways that *something* can go wrong that it's often wise to insure yourself against it.

Positive Black Swan Exposures

- Write a book
- Start a business (spending only what you can afford to lose)
- Make friends and connections
- Invent something
- Post your artwork on social media
- Perform at an open-mic night
- Explore lots of different ideas

STEP 1: Think about your exposure to negative black swans. What aspects of your life could be completely upended by something unforeseen?

STEP 2: Try to insulate yourself against those consequences. Can you buy insurance? Diversify your assets so a disaster in one area won't bankrupt you?

STEP 3: Pursue opportunities for positive black swans. See above for ideas.

☐ If you've exposed yourself to one positive black swan, or guarded against exposure to a negative one, check this box.

GROUP-PREVENT GROUPTHINK

In 1961, President Kennedy and his advisors launched an invasion of Cuba. It failed disastrously. Afterward, Kennedy's team identified their biggest problem: groupthink. Too eager to reach consensus, the group had stampeded in the wrong direction.

To stop that from reoccurring, Kennedy and his team worked out four rules for group decision-making. One year later, these rules helped them navigate the Cuban Missile Crisis, heading off the very real possibility of nuclear war.

Whether you're preventing World War III or deciding where to take a family vacation, these rules can help you maximize group brainpower.

STEP 1: Meet in an informal setting that doesn't belong to any one group member.

STEP 2: Have each member try to act as a "skeptical generalist," putting aside their personal focus in favor of an overall view.

STEP 3: Once you arrive at a plan, break into subgroups to come up with alternatives to it. Then get back together and present your results.

STEP 4: If your group has a boss, everybody else should sometimes meet without them, to make sure the boss's views don't dominate.

☐ If you've used President Kennedy's rules to prevent groupthink within a team, ask not what this win can do for you.

TIME IS MONEY—BUT HOW MUCH?

When you spend an hour bargain hunting, you end up with less time but more money. When you hire somebody to do chores for you, you end up with less money but more time.

Was either decision worth it? That depends on how much one minute of your life is worth.

There's no easy way to make the calculation. You could take your average hourly wage and apply that value to the rest of your life. But we value different hours differently. You'd have to be paid a lot more to work on your wedding day than on a random Tuesday.

When in doubt, save minutes rather than money; studies show that extra time makes you happier than extra cash.

That's why this exercise proposes several measures and suggests you take an average. Treat the result as a very rough guideline rather than a definitive answer.

STEP 1: Divide your annual after-tax take-home salary by the number of hours you work.

STEP 2: Think of a neutral chore you have to do—something you neither like nor dislike doing. What is the maximum you would pay somebody else to do it for an hour?

STEP 3: What is the minimum amount of money somebody would have to pay *you* to do an extra hour of that chore?

STEP 4: Add up the three numbers you got in the above steps. Divide by three to get a rough average estimate of how much you value your time.

SURFACE THE COST

Everything you do has a cost—in time, if not in money. It's easy to miss how quickly those costs add up. By **surfacing the cost** of an action, you can optimize your limited resources.

Common wisdom suggests cutting out little pleasures to save for big ones, but research suggests that lots of little pleasures will make you happier than one big one. That's why I recommend finding cost savings, rather than eliminating things you regularly enjoy.

STEP 1: Think of something you do often—shaving in the morning, for example, or buying coffee on the way to work.

STEP 2: Estimate how often you do it. Do you shave 365 days a year, or just on work days?

STEP 3: Estimate how much time and/or money each repetition costs you.

STEP 4: Multiply Step 3 by Step 2 to get your annual cost.

STEP 5: Consider ways to reduce the cost. It might be worth putting in an up-front investment. If a $300 coffee maker saves you $1 every day, it will pay for itself in ten months. If you spend an hour rearranging your bathroom to shave a minute off your morning shower (or to wash a minute off your morning shave), it will pay for itself in sixty days.

☐ If you've surfaced the cost of one regular action, you can afford a fraction of a second to acknowledge the win.

ZOOM IN ON THE VITAL FEW

The Pareto principle is a common rule of thumb in industry: 80 percent of the consequences come from 20 percent of the causes.

I call it a "rule of thumb" and not a law because life doesn't always break down into perfectly even percentages. But as a rough principle, it seems to apply widely. Microsoft found it could fix 80 percent of its crashes by fixing 20 percent of its bugs. And a study in New Zealand found that 22 percent of criminals accounted for 81 percent of convictions.

STEP 1: Think about an area of your life you want to optimize, like getting your kids out the door on school mornings.

STEP 2: Identify the **vital few**—the 20 percent that causes 80 percent of your problems. In my household, it's the moment before the kids go out the door and suddenly realize they're missing something from their schoolbag.

STEP 3: Fix that 20 percent.

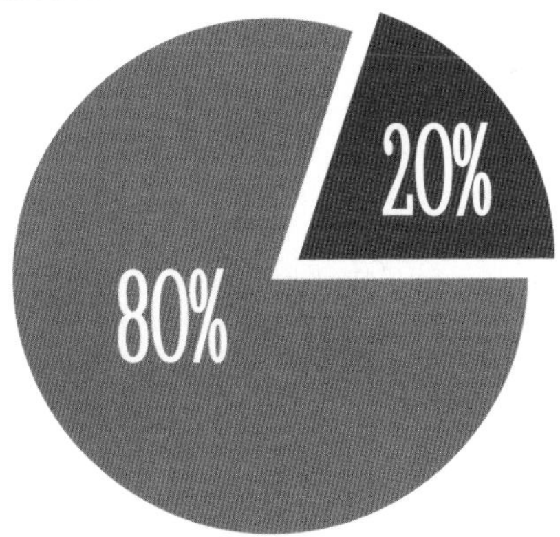

☐ If you've used the Pareto principle to zoom in on the vital few, you've zoomed in on a win.

BE YOUR OWN CHIEF OF STAFF

What do US presidents and CEOs of corporations have that you don't? Other than billions of dollars and control of the nuclear arsenal? A chief of staff.

Above all, a chief of staff makes sure their boss can focus on whatever is crucial at that very moment. To get things done, you need to think about what you're doing—not whether you should be doing it. To that end, a good chief of staff will:

- **Say "no" to things that don't advance the boss's priorities.**
- **Block out interruption-free time so the boss can do some in-depth thinking.**
- **Tell the boss when it's time to move on to the next thing so they can focus fully on this one.**
- **Keep a good to-do list (page 84).**

If you don't have a staff (let alone a chief of it), it's easy to let these things slide. Consciously choosing to be your own chief of staff can ensure you make them a priority.

One Thing You Can't Do for Yourself

On top of their other duties, a chief of staff provides daily accountability for somebody whose position on top of the food chain might make it otherwise hard to get. External accountability is one thing you can't do for yourself. Consider getting an accountability partner (page 102) to keep you honest.

STEP 1: Next time you're asked to do something, imagine you're setting the schedule for a boss who has your priorities. Would this go in your boss's calendar? If not, say no.

STEP 2: Put specific times and dates in your calendar to do the most important things. Set alarms to make sure you start and end at the right time.

STEP 3: If you have a hard time being your own chief of staff, set aside a specific time each week to do that duty. Use Pavlovian conditioning to put yourself in the right frame of mind (page 42).

☐ If thinking of yourself as your own chief of staff has helped you be more disciplined about sticking to priorities, have your chief of staff take the win.

MAKE AN UNDERWHELMING TO-DO LIST

Whatever battles you need to fight, your to-do list is a crucial weapon, but it's a frequently misunderstood one.

Consider this to-do list:

- ☐ *Become a movie star*

There's a pretty obvious problem with it: It doesn't tell you what to do. Let's make it a little more concrete:

- ☐ *Get an agent*
- ☐ *Prepare for auditions*
- ☐ *Go to auditions*
- ☐ *Repeat until I get the part*

We've now broken it down into specific steps. But if you woke up in the morning and the first item on your to-do list was "Get an agent," you'd be understandably overwhelmed. And at the end of the day, when you don't have a sunglasses-wearing hotshot making calls on your behalf, you'll feel like a failure—and you'll be less likely to try again tomorrow.

Let's break the list down into *next steps*, the lifeblood of any to-do list:

GET AN AGENT

- ☐ *Make a spreadsheet of agents I'm interested in*
- ☐ *Invite agents to* MAMMALTON, *my one-man musical about taxonomy*
- ☐ *Hire shills to give me a standing ovation*
- ☐ *Perform* MAMMALTON
- ☐ *Follow up with any agents who were there*

There's a trade-off here: The more concrete and specific each entry becomes, the bigger the to-do list grows. Personally, I like every item on my list to be achievable within a single Pomodoro session (page 99). You'll have to find your own balance, but the general goal is to fill your list with concrete things you can achieve right now. In fact, that's the philosophy of the entire Be Better Now series!

STEP 1: Break each of your strategic goals into broad steps.

STEP 2: Break each of those steps into concrete, actionable items.

STEP 3: If those items can't be done in a single day, break them down into next steps that can.

STEP 4: Keep breaking those steps down until you reach whatever level of detail makes you feel as if you can accomplish them.

☐ If everything on your to-do list is a concrete step you can take, then take the concrete step of accepting the win.

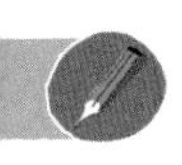

TICKLE YOURSELF

There are things you have to do at some point but aren't going to do now. Maybe you want a new sweater, but winter clothes aren't yet in shops. Whether you can't do a task or don't want to do it yet, you need a system that will bring them back to you at the right time.

In productivity-speak, that system is called a **tickler**.

In the days before everybody carried a supercomputer in their pockets, a tickler was a set of real-life paper folders. If you prefer a physical system (or if you just deal with a lot of physical papers), this is the approach for you. See the next page for tips on how to set it up.

If you'd rather do it electronically, you can set up a reminder app or just use your calendar app. Some to-do apps even have the built-in ability to add an item to your list at a future date, saving you the trouble of using an additional program. If that's the case, setting up a tickler system may be as simple as learning how to use this feature.

However you approach it, setting up a waiting room for future to-dos will leave your brain clearer for the stuff you need to do now.

STEP 1: Set up a tickler system, whether physical or electronic.

STEP 2: Even if your primary tickler is on your phone, you'll probably need some place to store paperwork you don't need yet. Set up a folder or a small box labeled "Stuff I Will Need on a Specific Future Date but Not Yet."

STEP 3: Review your to-do list. If you can't do anything on it today, transfer it to your tickler system.

Forty-three Folders

- Get forty-three folders and a file box to keep them in.
- Label twelve of the files with the months of the year. Put them in the box with next month at the front and the current month at the back. If it's March, your files will look like this.

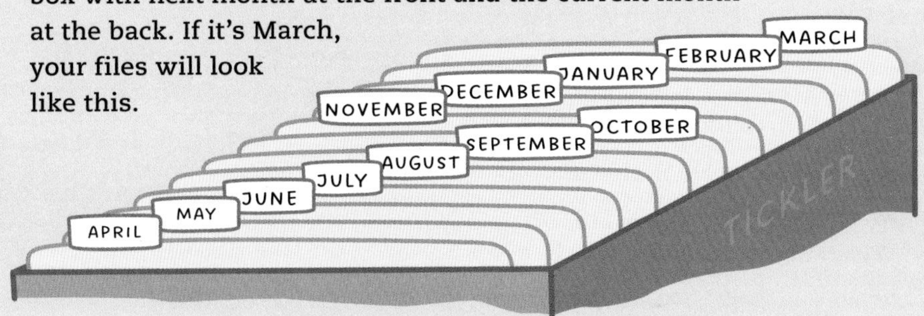

- Label the other folders with the numbers one through thirty-one. These will represent the days of the month. Put them at the very front of the box.
- Put each thing you need to do this month in the appropriate folder. That coupon that isn't active until the fourteenth? Put it in the fourteen folder.
- Now do the same for future months. Put bills in the month they're due (or in the month before that, if you want to be safe). Write *Birthday Present for Dad* on an index card, and put it in May. (Actual month may vary by dad.)
- Every morning you'll open your file and look at the folder for today's date. When you've done everything in it, you'll move it behind the other numbers. (For this reason, you don't need to make thirty-one separate folders for each month—you're reusing the same thirty-one day folders every month.)
- When you reach the end of March, you'll take everything out of the April folder, choose a date to do it on, and put it in the appropriate date folder. Then you'll put the April folder at the back of the month folders.

☐ If you've set up or used a tickler system, don't put off taking the win.

FOLLOW THE TWO-MINUTE RULE

To-do lists should be full of achievable action items—but some items are too achievable to bother writing down.

If you can get something done in two minutes, don't spend fifteen seconds writing it down. Just go ahead and do it.

Admittedly, productivity experts disagree on where the line is. Some advise a two-minute rule, and some suggest five. It may take some experimenting to find the time that works for you.

STEP 1: Next time you think of something you can do in two minutes, just do it, unless there's something specific stopping you.

STEP 2: If, and only if, there's something stopping you, put it on your to-do list.

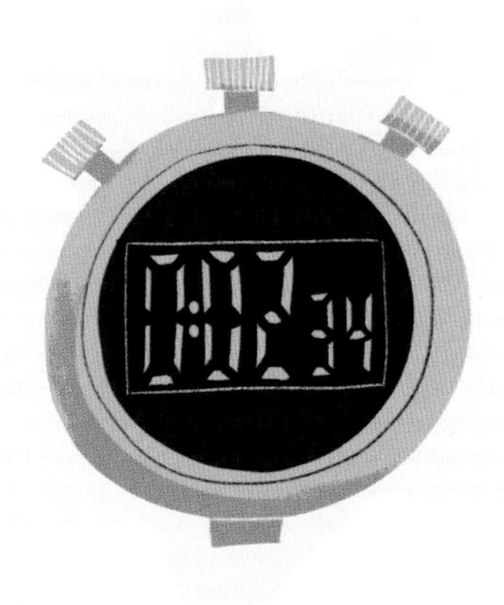

☐ If you've gotten one two-minute task done instead of putting it on your to-do list, spend a half second taking the win.

BUFF UP YOUR BRAIN

You know what a genius looks like: Wild hair. Rumpled clothes. Massive, rippling muscles.

Yes, I said muscles. Exercise enhances creativity, working memory, reasoning ability, and mental discipline, making this one tip that could go in any section of the book.

Brisk walking counts. "Exercise snacking"—running up the steps once, then doing it again a few hours later—counts. In fact, virtually any exercise is better than none. (Unless it involves blows to your skull. Stay away from heading a soccer ball or boxing.)

Long-term exercise gives you more available dopamine receptors, making you literally more capable of joy.

Ideally, you'll want to work up to an average of thirty minutes a day—but if you've done even five minutes, you're getting smarter already.

STEP 1: Do something that gets your body moving, whether it's an hour of intense swimming or five minutes of gardening.

STEP 2: If you have a creative task, try doing it while you're still feeling that post-exercise glow.

☐ If you've added even an extra five minutes of exercise to your day, add one more victory to your tally.

NO KUDOS TO PSEUDO TO-DOS

Look around the room. Do you see any of the following?

- **A kitchen catalog that you're saving to remind you to order a new colander.**
- **A bunch of books you ordered because you wanted to remember to read them.**
- **A Christmas card from your uncle that you left up when you put away the other Christmas cards so you'd remember to buy him a birthday present next May.**

If any of the above sounds familiar, you may be dependent on the **pseudo to-do list**. An actual to-do list is a written list of stuff you want to accomplish. A pseudo to-do list is a pile of stuff (physical or virtual). Unlike real to-do lists, pseudo to-dos are disorganized distractions that make your life *less* organized.

STEP 1: Choose one location for your actual to-do list. It could be a notebook, or a whiteboard, or an app on your phone.

STEP 2: Identify one pseudo to-do list you've accumulated, whether it's your overstuffed email inbox or that big pile of papers on your desk.

STEP 3: Methodically work your way through it. Convert each item into an entry on your actual to-do list, then move the item out of your way. Archive, respond to, or delete that email. Scan, recycle, or file that piece of paper, or put it in your tickler folder (page 86).

STEP 4: In the future, when new things come in, put them on your actual to-do list.

☐ If you've replaced one pseudo to-do list with a real one, give yourself a real win.

OUTSOURCE YOUR BRAIN INTO YOUR ENVIRONMENT

There's only so much stuff you can keep track of at once. Every second spent filing papers and paying bills reduces your focus on things you really care about.

Fortunately, you can take a number of steps to outsource routine cognitive tasks.

STEP 1: Sign up as many bills as you can for automatic bill paying.

STEP 2: Switch to electronic bank statements, so there's less paper to file.

STEP 3: For any object in your house that you have to look for more than once a month, pick a permanent place for it *and label that place* so you don't even have to spend the brainpower remembering that it goes there.

STEP 4: More generally, ask yourself if there are any repetitive tasks you can do with something other than your own brain. Instead of monitoring prices on that new lawnmower, can you sign up to for a price-comparison website?

☐ If you've outsourced any repetitive cognitive task, use the free time to celebrate your triumph.

DON'T GET KILLED ON COVERS

When you start a new task, your brain expends energy twice: first to get you in the right frame of mind, and then to do the task itself. It's like paying to get into a nightclub, and then paying to buy the drinks.

When you do five minutes of laundry, then file papers, and then spend ten minutes catching up on email, you're paying an extra cost every time you switch gears. That's like going to a different club for every drink. The cover charges are going to kill you.

Two Exceptions

Sometimes the cost of task-switching may be worth it—for example, when you're interleaving (page 4) or incubating (page 47).

STEP 1: Make a list of the tasks you want to get done.

STEP 2: Think about the mental processes involved in each one.

STEP 3: Group similar tasks together on your schedule. Some groupings will be obvious, like folding shirts and folding trousers. But should you follow up a business email with a personal email, or with a business call? Notice how different tasks feel to your particular brain.

☐ If you've grouped similar tasks together, whether in planning or in implementation, give yourself a win, a triumph, and a victory.

CHECKLIST? CHECK!

A checklist is a to-do list you use over and over again. It can be a literal lifesaver: one ICU found that using checklists prevented eight deaths over eighteen months. Pilots have known this for years; no jet takes off until the preflight checklist is completed.

Even when lives aren't at stake, a checklist can stop you from going on a business trip without a clean suit or waiting too long to start the gravy on Thanksgiving.

If you think you don't need one, ask yourself: Are you smarter than a surgeon? More detail-oriented than a pilot?

STEP 1: Identify a set of tasks you have to do repeatedly, especially one done under time pressure. It doesn't have to be daily. Even with annual events a checklist makes sure you don't forget the lessons learned one year by the time the next one rolls around.

STEP 2: In a calm moment, write down all the steps you need to do.

STEP 3: Post the checklist where it will be easily accessible at the right time, whether that's in a tickler folder (page 86) or right there in the box with the Thanksgiving decorations.

☐ If you've generated or used a checklist for a task you do often, add it to your list of victories.

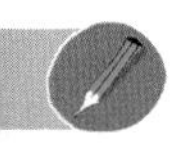

CONSERVE YOUR DECISION JUICE

As president, Barack Obama had to make world-changing decisions. He didn't have to decide what to wear. Every day, he'd put on either a gray suit or a blue suit. As he explained, "You need to focus your decision-making energy."

Obama was right: Decision-making energy can run out. In one study, parole judges freed 65 percent of prisoners when they started a session. But as the day dragged on, they resorted more often to the easy default of leaving prisoners in jail. By the end of a session, their decisions were almost 100 percent unfavorable.

Decision fatigue seems correlated to blood sugar. When the judges took a break for lunch, they returned refreshed and parole-friendly, once again ruling 65 percent in favor of prisoners.

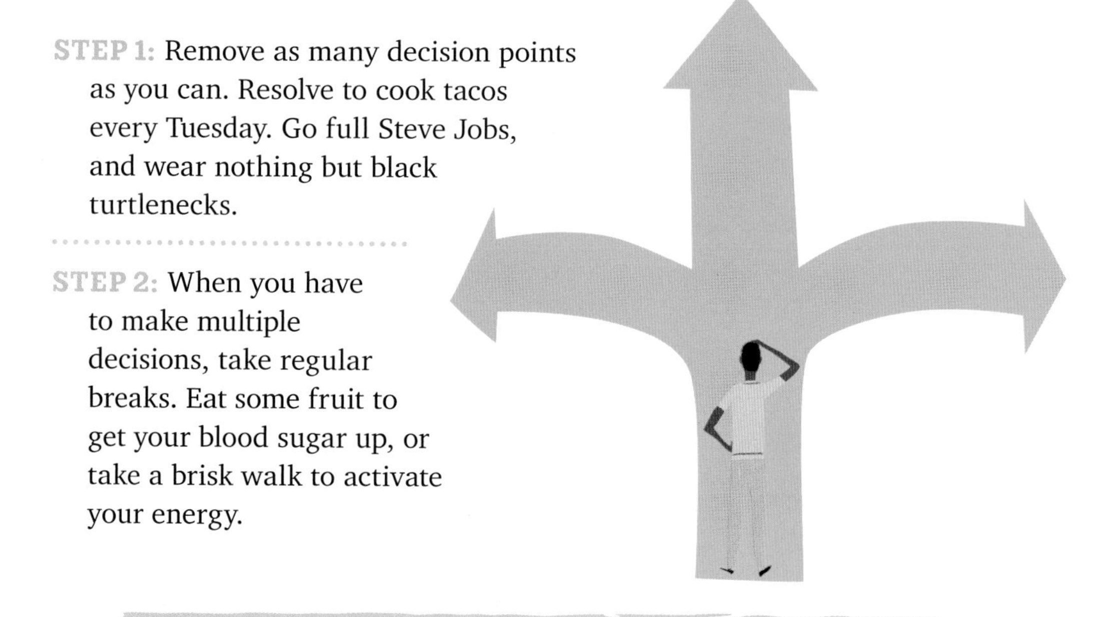

STEP 1: Remove as many decision points as you can. Resolve to cook tacos every Tuesday. Go full Steve Jobs, and wear nothing but black turtlenecks.

STEP 2: When you have to make multiple decisions, take regular breaks. Eat some fruit to get your blood sugar up, or take a brisk walk to activate your energy.

☐ If you've taken one step to avoid decision fatigue, give yourself the win without even thinking about it.

Do Smarter is about tactical intelligence—transforming your plans into real-world action. From good habits to end-of-day rituals, *Do Smarter* has what you need to act on all your brilliant plans.

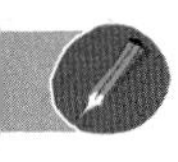

STACK GOOD HABITS ON TOP OF OLD HABITS

In a perfect life, there are some things you hope to do only occasionally (like buying a house) or even once (like getting married). Everything else is some form of habit.

What creates a habit? Psychologists say it's the cycle of *trigger*, *action*, and *reward*.

STEP 1: Identify a habit you want to acquire, like doing ten push-ups every day.

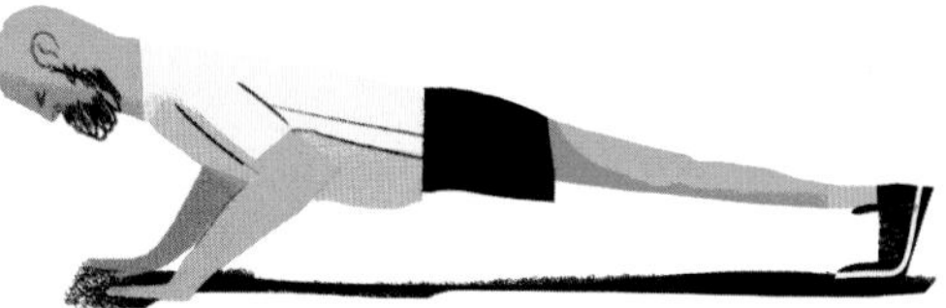

STEP 2: Choose a trigger for the habit. Ideally, this will be some concrete thing you already do regularly, like walking into your office at Wayne Enterprises. Stacking a new habit on top of an old one can be very effective.

STEP 3: Think about a reward your new habit will lead to. This might be something you'll experience immediately afterward (like the endorphin rush from exercising) or a long-term goal (like having the upper-body strength to punch Gotham's criminals).

STEP 4: Do your desired action as soon as the trigger occurs. Afterward, luxuriate for a moment in the reward (if it's something immediate) or the anticipation of the reward (if it's more long term).

☐ If you've given yourself a trigger and a reward for a good habit, consider it a triumph.

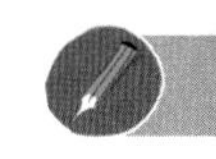

DESTROY THE TRIGGERS

The good thing about many habits is that you do them automatically. The bad thing about many habits is that you do them automatically. Good or bad, psychologists call that **automaticity**. Thanks to automaticity, breaking bad habits can be harder than creating good ones—but it's a challenge worth taking on.

To learn more, read *The Power of Habit* by Charles Duhigg.

STEP 1: Choose a habit you want to break. (Serious physical addictions like smoking are probably beyond the reach of this method.)

STEP 2: Identify the triggers that set you off. Do you automatically open Twitter when you sit down in a specific chair?

STEP 3: Avoid those triggers. Sit in a different chair that you don't associate with Twitter. Even holding the phone in your other hand may work.

STEP 4: Identify the **positive reinforcement** you get from the habit. Maybe it's the little burst of approval you get when somebody likes your posts.

STEP 5: Find an alternative way to get that positive reinforcement. If you're seeking approval, can you email your always-encouraging big sister instead?

HI, SIS!

☐ If you've broken the routine that leads to a bad habit, or found a healthier way to get positive reinforcement, pat yourself on the back.

GIVE GOOD HABITS ENOUGH TIME TO SETTLE IN

How long does it take to reach **maximum automaticity**—that magical stage where a habit is as automatic as it's going to get?

It varies from person to person and habit to habit. One study found that maximum automaticity can take as few as 18 days or as many as 254 days, with an average time of 66 days. The more complex the habit, the longer it's likely to take. Think of these numbers as a general guideline—a reminder that change isn't always quick, but it is possible.

STEP 1: Think of a habit you're trying to acquire.

STEP 2: Get out your calendar and count 18 days from when you first started. Mark that as "Earliest automaticity." (Or "Earliest habit date," if your habit is "Stop using overly fancy words.") Count 66 days from your start, and mark that "Average automaticity." Count 254 days (or about eight and a half months), and mark that "Latest automaticity."

STEP 3: Every day you stick with your habit, cross off one square on your calendar. Feel yourself getting closer to making it automatic.

☐ If you've tracked one habit, add another victory to your tally.

TOMATO!

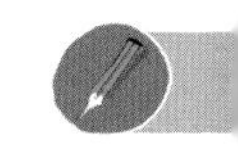

Decades ago, a student named Francesco Cirillo found a simple way to overcome procrastination. He broke his work into unintimidating twenty-five-minute chunks, which he measured with a tomato-shaped kitchen timer. He called it the Pomodoro technique, from the Italian word for "tomato."

I'm a lifelong procrastinator, and the fact that you're reading my eleventh published book is a testament to the surprising power of this simple technique.

STEP 1: Set a timer for twenty-five minutes.

STEP 2: Keep working while the timer is ticking. Remind yourself that you can check your email or scroll Facebook *after* the current Pomodoro is done.

STEP 3: When the timer *dings*, give yourself five minutes of goofing off. Then reset the timer and dive into another twenty-five-minute session.

STEP 4: Every four sessions, let yourself take a longer break. Cirillo suggests twenty or thirty minutes.

STEP 5: Adjust the timing to suit your own working style.

☐ If you've used the Pomodoro technique to get things done, give yourself the win.

BECOME MORE EFFICIENT BY WANDERING THROUGH THE WOODS

If you can't stay focused, you might be suffering from **ego depletion**—a state in which you just don't have the mental resources to pay attention. One way to recharge is to spend time in nature. In the short term, it's been shown to improve focus. In the long term, people who habitually spend time in nature are less likely to procrastinate.

One possible explanation is that natural environments are full of things that draw your attention pleasantly and easily, freeing you of the need to focus consciously, and giving your brain time to recover. Or maybe nature is simply good for the soul.

Whatever the reason, time spent connecting with nature can add to, rather than take away from, the time you spend getting stuff done.

Spending time in nature reduces stress and lowers your risk of depression.

STEP 1: Connect with nature however you can. If there are woods nearby, take a walk through them. If not, consider planting a garden, or even contemplating the houseplant on your desk.

STEP 2: When you're feeling refreshed, dive back into your work.

☐ If you've connected with nature, harvest a victory.

THE PERFECT OFFICE ENVIRONMENT?

HIDE YOUR PHONE

A smartphone can have all sorts of brain-boosting functions. You can use it to help you learn facts (page 9) or strengthen your working memory (page 34).

But it can also be a distraction—even when you're not using it. Studies have shown that people are more error-prone when they have a turned-off cell phone in their range of vision. Turning off notifications (page 108) stops you from being actively interrupted, but it doesn't stop your brain from thinking about all the cool distracting things you could be doing with your phone.

Having a face-to-face conversation without a cell phone in sight can increase feelings of emotional connection.

STEP 1: If you're doing complex work that requires focus, move your phone someplace you can't see or feel it.

☐ If you've moved your cell phone out of sight to help you focus, move a trophy into your field of vision.

GET AN ACCOUNTABILITY PARTNER

We often take assignments more seriously when they come from somebody else. We don't want to disappoint the people who believe in us. In a variation of the fundamental attribution error (page 128), we can assume that somebody else's commands spring from inherent knowledge we don't have. And sometimes we simply defer to authority.

Fortunately, you can make these mental quirks work for you.

STEP 1: Choose a goal that will require sustained effort.

STEP 2: Make a deal with a friend to hold you accountable. Agree that you will report your progress to them at regular, predetermined intervals. If they don't hear from you, they should contact you and ask for a progress report.

STEP 3: You can ask them to give you a specific goal for your next report, or even tell them what goal to give you. Either way, they should have a concrete, measurable goal to hold you to, and you should feel that they hold the reins.

☐ If you've worked with a partner to hold yourself accountable, you've both won.

MAKE A TO-DONE LIST

I'm a big believer in to-do lists (page 84), but they're never-ending. Floors refuse to stay vacuumed. And no matter how many bills I pay, they keep sending me new ones.

That's why I sometimes luxuriate in a to-done list. A to-done list is like a to-do list, but every thing on it is something I've already done. What could be more encouraging?

Self-indulgent as a to-done list might feel, it has real practical benefits. A feeling of progress is a crucial source of **intrinsic motivation**—an inner desire to get something done.

STEP 1: If a task seems overwhelming, list the things you've already done.

STEP 2: Include things you already checked off a to-do list, as well as things you didn't think to put on the to-do list. Make sure you give yourself credit for steps that felt easy or intuitive to you. By definition, those are the things you've mastered, and shouldn't you get credit for mastery?

☐ If you've put together a to-done list, mark *this* task as to-done.

EAT A LIVE FROG

For decades, I've been quoting Mark Twain: "Eat a live frog first thing in the morning, and nothing worse will happen to you all day."

Alas, in researching this book, I discovered that Mark Twain never said those words. Admitting that I'm wrong is deeply unpleasant, and it might be why I've put off writing this entry until I'm done with almost the entire book.

But now that I've gotten it off my chest, I feel a tremendous sense of relief, and nothing is holding me back from finishing this page.

That's why "Eat the frog" is common advice to cure procrastination. We often put off a task because of its most unpleasant aspect. If we dive in and get the worst out of the way, the rest seems easy.

It's like Mark Twain always said: "Misquote Mark Twain first thing in the morning, and nothing more embarrassing will happen to you all day."

STEP 1: If there's a task you've been putting off, identify the most unpleasant aspect of it.

STEP 2: Do it immediately, before you have the chance to worry about it anymore.

STEP 3: Enjoy the rest of the day.

☐ If you've started your day with your most dreaded task, give yourself the more pleasant task of taking the win.

MASTER A MIME MNEMONIC

Retrospective memory allows you to remember things you learned and stuff you did. **Prospective memory** allows you to remember stuff you want to do in the future.

If you can't remember what groceries you were supposed to buy, blame your retrospective memory. But if you forgot to go to the store in the first place, you have prospective memory problems.

Fortunately, there's a solution. It's called **enactment**, and it's based on a principle we encountered on page 42: Neurons that fire together wire together. By miming the thing you want to remember while imagining the time you want to do it, you create neural associations that trigger the memory at the right moment.

Sound implausible? Watch Olympic skiers preparing for a run. Their eyes closed, they sway back and forth, miming the actions they're about to take. If enactment helps them zip down a hill at ninety-five miles an hour, it can certainly help you walk into Kroger.

STEP 1: Choose an action you want to perform in the future, like "Get milk."

STEP 2: Imagine the situation in which you should perform it. Picture yourself walking down the street to the grocery store. Hear the sound of the street, and smell the exhaust of the passing cars.

STEP 3: Now mime out the actions. As you imagine walking into the store, lift your feet and walk in place. As you imagine pulling milk off the shelf, lift up your real-life hand.

☐ If you've used an enactment cue to remember to do one thing, act out a victory dance.

WORK LESS TO ACCOMPLISH MORE

Imagine two teams. Team Grindstone works sixty hours a week. Team Coffee Break works forty. After a couple of months, Team Coffee Break might be happier and better rested, but you know who got more done?

Also Team Coffee Break.

Studies show that lack of rest is a major cause of inefficiency. Staying late to make one extra widget today can mean you'll make two fewer widgets tomorrow. Cheat on rest long enough and your productivity becomes *negative*—you end up breaking two widgets for every one you make.

Inside an overworked system, people are often too exhausted to notice the damage exhaustion does. But when businesses bring in outside experts to study their workers, the results are consistent: People who work forty to fifty hours a week accomplish more in the long run than people who work more than sixty hours. Not just more per hour: more, period.

Reducing hours further may lead to even more gains. When Microsoft Japan went from a five-day workweek to a four-day one, productivity improved 40 percent.

The one exception is for short-term crunches. If you have a deadline in the next month or two, you may find you can pull a couple of sixty-hour weeks. But if you try to keep that schedule beyond that, you'll end up worse off than if you had just stuck with forty-hour weeks all along. If you do force yourself to work overtime for a crunch, try to schedule some vacation time afterward.

STEP 1: Add up your working hours.

STEP 2: If you're working more than fifty hours a week, definitely cut back. If you're working between forty and fifty hours, try cutting back to forty as an experiment. If you're working forty, try thirty-five. You might find you get as much or more done in a shorter amount of time.

STEP 3: If you're forced to work more than fifty hours a week, be kind to yourself. Under those circumstances, lack of perfect efficiency isn't a failure. It's human nature.

- [ ] If you've worked fewer than fifty hours this week, spend a few moments acknowledging the win.

TURN OFF YOUR NOTIFICATIONS

You've cleared off your schedule. You're ready to concentrate on some important task with a laserlike focus. Now all you have to do is—

DING! NEW EMAIL!

Sorry. All you have to do is—

INCOMING MESSAGE: COUPON CODE FOR FREE PIZZA!

All you—

DING! NEW LEVEL AVAILABLE FOR *NINJA FRUIT QUEST!*

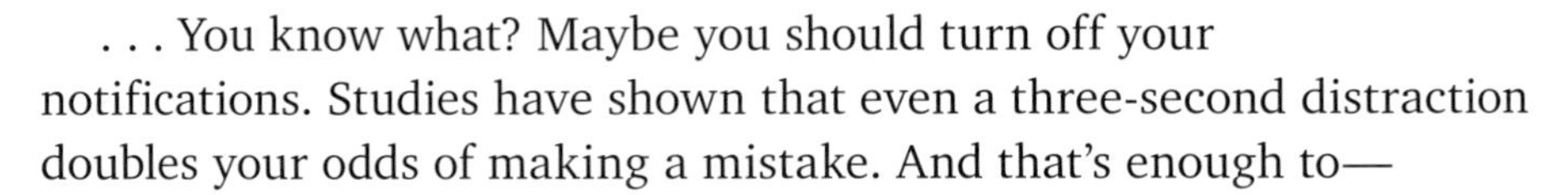

. . . You know what? Maybe you should turn off your notifications. Studies have shown that even a three-second distraction doubles your odds of making a mistake. And that's enough to—

DING! NEWS UPDATE: CONGRESS DECLARES AUGUST "NO DISTRACTIONS MONTH"!

STEP 1: Go to the notifications settings on your phone. Turn every single one off.

STEP 2: Now go through them again, and for each one, follow the flow chart.

STEP 3: Repeat this process for your computer, your tablet, and any other device you regularly use.

STEP 4: Whenever you install a new app, get in the habit of clicking "No" when it asks if it can notify you.

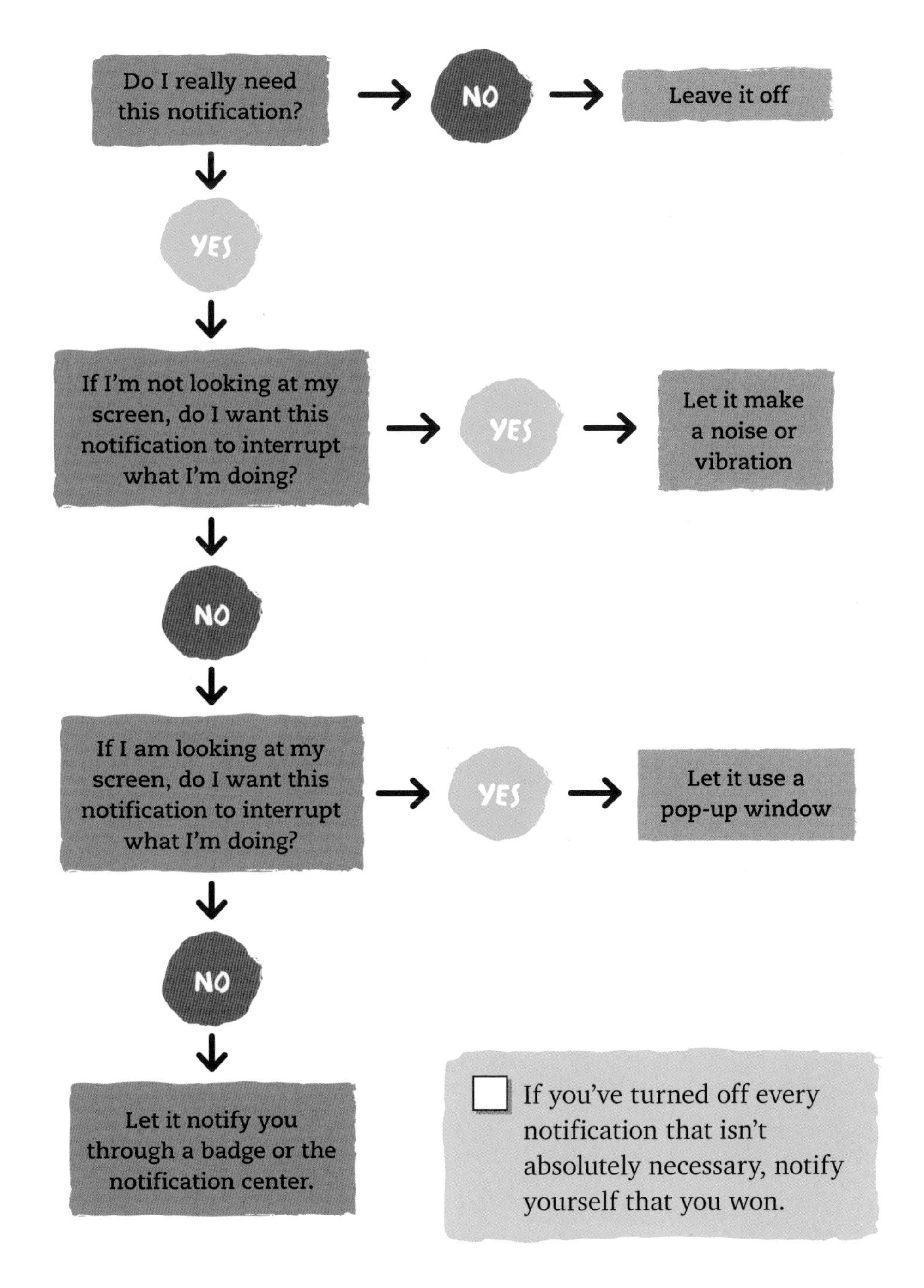

Do I really need this notification?
NO
Leave it off
YES
If I'm not looking at my screen, do I want this notification to interrupt what I'm doing?
YES
Let it make a noise or vibration
NO
If I am looking at my screen, do I want this notification to interrupt what I'm doing?
YES
Let it use a pop-up window
NO
Let it notify you through a badge or the notification center.
If you've turned off every notification that isn't absolutely necessary, notify yourself that you won.

GET LESS ORGANIZED

Legends speak of a fabled land known as Inbox Zero, where emails are responded to immediately and you don't have to hunt for important messages among the forest of Things I Already Read but Haven't Yet Sorted into Folders.

You may never set eyes upon this land, but you can take steps to get yourself closer. One is to stop using your inbox as a to-do list (see page 90). Another is this:

Stop organizing your emails.

Once upon a time, when your computer was steam-powered and searching for a keyword took fifteen minutes, it made sense to laboriously sort emails from your best friend Ronit into their own folder. But now, if you need to find that gulab jamun recipe he sent you, it's faster to just type "Ronit gulab jamun" into the search bar.

It's surprisingly liberating to stop trying to organize your email. More important, you can use the time you save to make me gulab jamun. Just send it in care of the publisher.

STEP 1: Figure out which emails you *don't* need to sort into folders. Pretty much any email folder with somebody's name on it is unnecessary. If you want to find all the emails your aunt sent you—well, her name is already on every email she sent, just waiting for the search function.

STEP 2: Figure out which emails you *do* need to sort into folders. These are the emails where the keyword isn't already included in every message. If you need to find all the messages from people you met through your roller derby team, you can't just type "Badass Chicks On Skates." That might justify a folder.

STEP 3: Create a folder called "Archive." (Some email systems will already have this as standard.) This is where you'll store every email that doesn't have its own dedicated folder.

STEP 4: Learn your email program's shortcut to archive emails. Often, it only takes a single swipe or a single command key.

STEP 5: If you've already spent hours organizing your email folders, you don't need to empty them. But as new messages come in, archive them as a default. Only file the ones that really need it.

- [ ] If you've archived emails instead of laboriously sorting them into folders, consider it a triumph.

DON'T DISTRACT YOURSELF

Earlier, I talked about the cognitive cost of doing different kinds of tasks one after the other (page 92). If it's mentally inefficient to do one thing for ten minutes and then a different thing for ten minutes, imagine how much worse it is to do both things at once.

That's assuming you *can* do two things at once. What most people call multitasking actually involves rapidly switching back and forth between tasks. Each switch takes time and mental energy. Even when that time is brief, it can add up. And sometimes it can be deadly: In the time it takes you to shift your attention from a text message to the road in front of you, your car can plunge off the highway.

In certain situations, where creativity is more important than efficiency and there's no life-or-death need for concentration, multitasking may work in your favor (see page 48). But when concentration and efficiency matter, monotasking is the better option.

STEP 1: For anything that requires mental concentration, find a time to do it when you won't be doing something else.

☐ If you've focused on one thing rather than multitasking, focus intently on your victory.

FLIP IT AND REVERSE IT

You can spend an hour hunting for missing keys, only to discover they were sitting on your living room table in plain sight. You can read the same line over and over again and never catch the typo.

In both cases, your brain stubbornly refuses to focus on details. Fortunately, there's a way to force your brain to snap to attention. By breaking your mental routine, you can cause **disfluency**, forcing your brain to proceed more slowly and carefully.

Ways to Break Routine

- When you're rereading something you've written, find ways to make the experience different. Change your document to a strange font. Or use a text-to-speech function to *listen* to your document.
- If you're copying your driver's license number onto a form, check the digits in the reverse order from which you entered them.
- When looking for something, many people instinctively move their eyes in the same direction they read. Try scanning from right to left instead.

STEP 1: When you do something that requires close attention to detail, find a way to break your mental routine. See the above for some examples.

☐ If you've forced yourself to pay attention by creating disfluency, pat your back with your nondominant hand.

ESTABLISH AN ELECTORAL COLLEGE

I drew most of this book from scientific research or the firsthand accounts of people who are smarter than I am. If you'll indulge me, I want to offer something I stumbled onto myself:

My wife and I express our opinions by convening an imaginary electoral college. We each can send up to one hundred delegates, and they'll vote however we tell them. A conversation might go something like this:

"What do you want to order for dinner tonight?"

"Fifty-one of my delegates vote for Chinese food and forty-seven vote for pizza."

"Sixty-four of my delegates vote for Indian."

"Indian it is!"

Silly though this is, it has three advantages.

First, it offers a great deal of nuance. If ten of my delegates vote for something, it means, "This is an okay option for me, but it's not great." Fifty-one of my delegates means, "This is my first choice, but just barely." One hundred delegates means, "I feel more strongly about this than anything else in my entire life."

Second, it helps us find compromise options. In the example above, if pizza had been my wife's second choice, she could have tipped the election to it with a mere eighteen delegates.

Third, the silliness is actually a strength. It stops us from taking minor disagreements too seriously.

STEP 1: If you and a friend have different preferences, and there's no objective reason to choose one over the other, convene an electoral college. (You can do this with multiple friends, too. It just requires a little bit more math.)

STEP 2: Think about the options you'd be happy with. The more strongly you feel about a choice, the more delegates you should assign to it.

STEP 3: You can't send more than one hundred delegates, but it's fine to send fewer. If you don't feel passionately, some of your delegates can skip the vote.

STEP 4: Reveal your votes. Add up the totals. Whichever option has the most votes carries the convention.

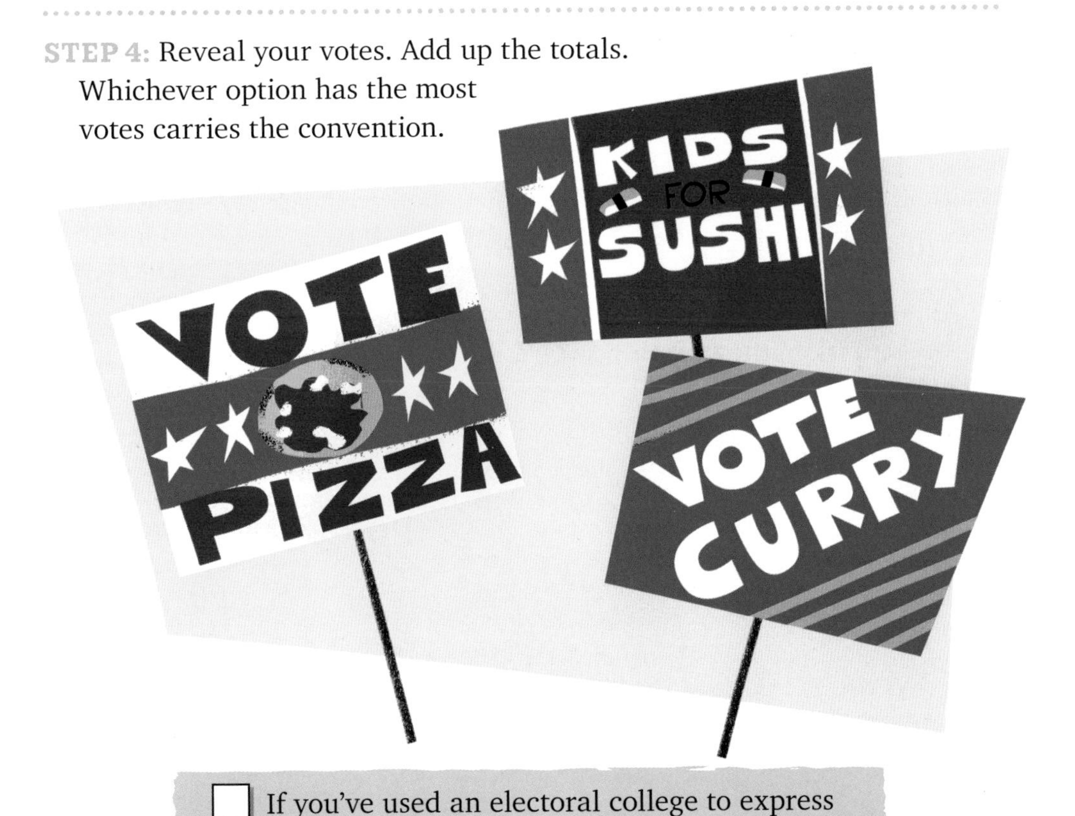

☐ If you've used an electoral college to express preference, vote yourself the victor.

END TODAY BY SETTING YOURSELF UP FOR TOMORROW

Days are more productive when you can dive straight into the task at hand. Rather than waste those productive early hours cleaning off your desk and figuring out your plan, do those tasks at the end of the day, when your brain is already too tired for real work.

STEP 1: At the end of the day, clean up your physical work area. Clean up your virtual work area, too—close any tabs you don't need.

STEP 2: Set your priorities for tomorrow. Most important, decide the first thing you'll do the next morning; that will set the tone for the day.

STEP 3: Write down your plan for the next day somewhere you'll be sure to see it. I have a whiteboard on the outside of my home office door.

STEP 4: If your software allows it, set up your computer so that when you turn it on, the first thing you'll see is the document or app you want to start with.

STEP 5: Shut down your computer, turn off your office lights, and switch off your work brain for the day.

☐ If you've ended your day with a productive routine, consider it a triumph.

Reason Smarter is about your logical, deductive mind. From finding the optimal amount of data to understanding probabilities, *Reason Smarter* will help you unleash your inner Sherlock Holmes.

MEDITATE

For millennia, meditation has been seen as a path to wisdom. Laboratory study of it is more recent. Scientists have found preliminary but compelling evidence that regular meditation changes your brain, with benefits including an increased ability to focus your attention.

If you'd like guidance from an experienced teacher, sign up for a local class or download a meditation app. If you'd like to give it a go on your own, try the exercise below.

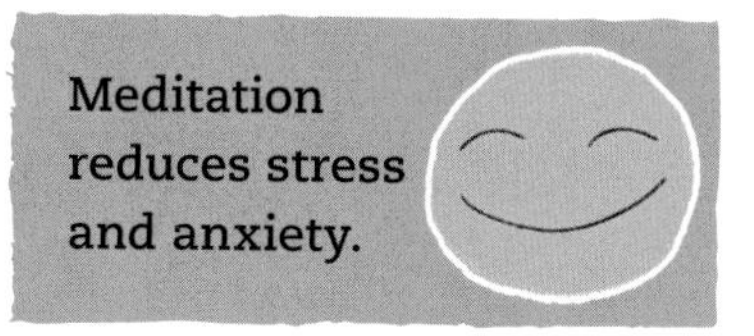

STEP 1: Sit comfortably in a quiet place with no distractions.

STEP 2: Close your eyes. Feel your breath flowing in and out. Notice how your chest rises and falls. If your mind wanders, don't worry—that's natural. Just calmly and without judgment bring your attention back to your breath.

STEP 3: Let your attention flow to your feet. Notice, without judgment, what sensations they are feeling. Let your attention flow upward, scanning your body until you reach the top of your head.

NARROW YOUR FOCUS

If you've ever stood in a grocery store aisle, unable to come to a decision while comparing calories, fat, and sugar content of multiple brands, you've experienced **analysis paralysis**. You've learned that more information isn't always better.

Based on psychological studies, the optimum number of factors for a single decision seems to be about five. And once you get beyond ten, decision-making doesn't just get harder—it actually gets worse, as you get distracted from the crucial facts by more and more irrelevancies.

Interestingly, it doesn't seem to matter how those factors are divided. If you're choosing between two chocolate bars, you can compare them on five different factors. If you're choosing among five chocolate bars, you're better off stopping at two questions about each.

STEP 1: Think about a decision you need to make.

STEP 2: Try narrowing your decision down to five comparisons. If you just can't do that, narrow it down to no more than ten.

STEP 3: If you can't narrow it down immediately, try dividing your choices into two groups and deciding between them. Rather than try to compare twenty houses across two neighborhoods, start by comparing the two neighborhoods. With only two things to compare, you can handle five different comparisons between them. Once you've chosen that neighborhood, there might be five houses in it. Pick just two factors, and decide among the houses based on that.

☐ If you've made a decision by narrowing your focus, zoom in on the victory.

DO SOME MORAL ALGEBRA

English scientist Joseph Priestley was one of the great minds of the eighteenth century. But he encountered a challenge that resisted scientific analysis: Should he take a promising job in another city? He wrote to one of the few people who might have been smarter than him: Ben Franklin.

What makes decisions difficult, Franklin wrote back, is that "all the Reasons *pro* and *con* are not present to the Mind at the same time; but sometimes one Set present themselves, and at other times another, the first being out of Sight." Franklin suggested a procedure to help Priestley get his head around everything simultaneously. He called it "Moral or Prudential Algebra." It's an ingenious way of cutting back the number of factors in a decision (see previous page).

Priestley decided to take the job, leading to a period of remarkable scientific achievement that included the discovery of oxygen.

STEP 1: Take out a piece of paper and draw a line in the middle. Label one half "pros" and the other "cons."

STEP 2: Write down all the pros and cons you can think of, but don't make any decisions yet. Keep the paper handy for the next few days, writing down more pros and cons whenever they occur to you.

STEP 3: When you can't think of any more pros or cons, start thinking about the importance of each one—what Franklin called their "Respective Weights". If you find one particular pro that's as important as one particular con, cross them both out. If there's one con that's as important as three pros, cross out all four.

STEP 4: Eventually, it should become clear whether the pros outweigh the cons or vice versa.

☐ If you've used Franklin's method to help you make one decision, give yourself the win.

TAKE IT LYING DOWN

"You won't catch me napping" is considered a boast, but it should be a shameful admission. Brief afternoon naps have been clinically proven to improve alertness, learning ability, and reasoning skills. Even if you got a great night's sleep, you might benefit from a short nap.

STEP 1: When you feel a midday drop in energy, get ready to nap. For many people, this will be some time between 11 AM and 4 PM.

STEP 2: One study found maximum benefits from ten minutes of dozing. It takes roughly ten minutes to fall asleep, so set an alarm for twenty minutes after you lie down. Depending on how it goes, you can modify future naptimes.

STEP 3: Get in bed, or put your head down on the desk.

STEP 4: If you drink caffeine in the afternoon, experiment with having it right before you lie down. You might find that it hits your bloodstream just as your alarm goes off, letting you bounce right into action.

STEP 5: Doze.

STEP 6: When you get up, ease into wakefulness with two or three minutes of gentle stretching or walking.

☐ If you've taken an afternoon nap, wake up to victory.

GET WIRED

Most drugs that boost your brain come with such serious side effects I can't recommend them. One exception? Caffeine, in the form of coffee and tea. In the short term, caffeine helps you focus and may increase your ability to reason. In the long term, moderate regular coffee consumption is correlated with a reduced risk of neurological diseases like Parkinson's or Alzheimer's, while tea (especially green tea) is a rich source of healthy antioxidants.

One caution: The American Academy of Sleep Medicine recommends that you stay away from caffeine for six hours before you hit the hay.

Coffee and tea drinkers are less likely to suffer from depression.

STEP 1: Make coffee or tea.

STEP 2: Resist the urge to add too much sugar or cream. If you can't quit them cold turkey, try to gradually reduce the amount you add to your cup.

☐ If you've had a cup of coffee or tea, toast your win.

ASK THE RIGHT QUESTIONS

Which kills more people: hepatitis, terrorism, or natural disasters? Don't worry if you don't know—just make your best guess before reading on.

You probably don't have an intimate familiarity with worldwide mortality figures. And so, consciously or unconsciously, you likely answered a different, easier question. Maybe you asked yourself, "Which cause of death am I most afraid of?" or "Which cause of death have I seen on the news most recently?" If so, you likely answered "terrorism" or "natural disasters."

Alas, you were wrong. Hepatitis kills more people than terrorism and natural disasters combined.

You've just fallen prey to the **availability heuristic**—the tendency to confuse "Leaps readily into my mind" with "Happens more often." Don't feel bad; if you were the only one who did it, psychologists wouldn't have a fancy, multisyllabic name for it.

Sometimes swapping in an easier question works. For example, which German city do you think is bigger: Berlin or Bielefeld? If you don't know, make a guess before reading on.

Most likely, you thought something like, "I'm more likely to have heard of a big city than a small one. So which city have I heard of?" Unless you're a lifelong Bielefeldian, your answer was "Berlin." Congratulations! You're absolutely right.

You can't always stop your mind from swapping questions—it often happens automatically in the background. But you can learn to recognize the process. Doing so will help ensure that you're answering the right questions.

STEP 1: Next time you encounter a question you don't know, see if a guess pops into your head. (Quick: How many dogs are there in America?)

STEP 2: Notice your guess. Consciously or unconsciously, did you answer a substitute question? Instead of "How many dogs are there?" did you answer, "What's a big number I can think of quickly?" That's probably *not* a great substitute question.

STEP 3: Try to find a better substitute question. "How many dogs are in America?" might become, "What percentage of Americans own dogs?"

Estimating Hard Questions by Asking Easy Questions

GOOD SUBSTITUTIONS

- How many gas stations are there in America? →
  - How many people are there in America?
  - What percentage of people have cars?
  - On average, how many cars can one gas station serve?
- Roughly when was *Casablanca* filmed? →
  - When was World War II?
- Who are the bestselling bands of all time? →
  - What bands has everybody I know heard of, across multiple generations?

BAD SUBSTITUTIONS

- Is this person dangerous? →
  - Does this person look like the bad guy in the last movie I saw?
- Is it safe to smoke cigarettes? →
  - Do I know one smoker who lived to be a hundred?
- Does everybody in the world hold a certain belief? →
  - Does everybody I follow on social media hold this belief?

☐ If you've consciously substituted an easy question for a hard one—or checked yourself from doing it unconsciously—ask yourself, "Do I deserve credit for this?"

SHOOT DOWN SURVIVORSHIP BIAS

In 1943, the Pentagon examined airplanes returning from combat. They proposed adding extra armor to the fuselage and wings, where most of the bullet holes were. Statistician Abraham Wald had a better idea: Armor the motor, because it had the *fewest* holes.

As Wald had realized, the Pentagon was guilty of **survivorship bias**. They were only paying attention to the planes that came back. Wald thought about the ones that didn't. Those were the ones that had taken bullets to their motors . . . which meant that armoring the motor was the best way to bring flyboys home alive.

It's easy to fall prey to survivorship bias. We hear about successful filmmakers who charged their entire first film to a credit card and forget about unsuccessful filmmakers who are stuck with massive debt. We watch a YouTube video with a cancer survivor who ignored medical advice, and we don't notice the patients who are a little too dead for social media.

STEP 1: Think about a lesson you've learned from somebody else's success—or even your own.

STEP 2: Ask yourself: What should you know about the people who *didn't* succeed? How can you expand your knowledge?

☐ If you've avoided one instance of survivorship bias in your own life, consider yourself the victor.

BREATHE BETTER TO THINK BETTER

The air you breathe affects your intelligence. Bad enough pollution can eventually cause long-term brain damage equivalent to losing an entire year of education.

Even when we breathe in clean air, we breathe out carbon dioxide. Without proper ventilation, the amount of carbon dioxide in an ordinary boardroom or classroom can be enough to temporarily impair your reasoning and decision-making.

STEP 1: Check your local air quality at airnow.gov. If it's bad, get an air filter. Look for a HEPA filter if possible.

STEP 2: If the outside air quality is good, leave a window open to let in fresh air.

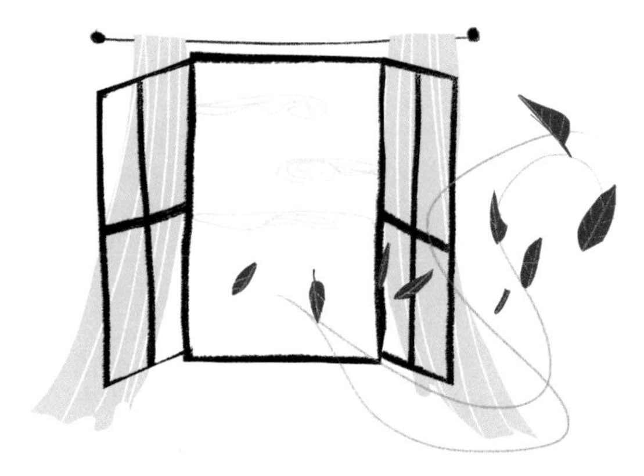

STEP 3: If you live in a polluted area, you may have to choose between closing windows (and letting carbon dioxide build up) or opening them (and letting pollution in). Consider opening the windows at night, when pollution is often lower. Or open the windows to let fresh air in, then close them and run a filter to clean it. At the very least, keep as many internal doors open as possible so the carbon dioxide doesn't build up in any one room.

☐ If you've improved your air quality, breathe in your triumph.

SEE PEOPLE IN CONTEXT

I cut people off in traffic because I'm in a rush. People cut me off because they're jerks.

Forgetting that other people's actions are shaped by circumstances is called the **fundamental attribution error**. It makes us think a cabbie is hostile (when we just caught them on a bad day) or a quiz show host is smart (when they're just reading the answers).

With a bit of thought, you can judge your fellow human beings more accurately.

STEP 1: Think of a conclusion you reached about somebody else's nature.

STEP 2: Ask yourself: How could circumstances have shaped the behavior you observed?

STEP 3: Think about times in which you've behaved that way. Was your behavior a result of your fundamental nature, or was it shaped by circumstances?

STEP 4: Next time you're tempted to reach a conclusion about somebody's fundamental nature, defer judgment until you have a quiet moment to reflect on their circumstances. Studies show you're more likely to fall into the fundamental attribution error when you're feeling information overload.

HONK! HONK! HONK!

☐ If you've put one person's behavior in context, put yourself on the winner's podium.

BRING IN THE OUT-GROUP

You're more likely to recognize nuance within your **in-group**—the group you belong to. As a hard-rocking headbanger, you know metalheads of all different types . . . but classical fans are a bunch of snobs. Meanwhile, your local orchestra conductor thinks you rowdy metalheads are all alike.

Our difficulty in comprehending **out-groups** is a major problem for society. One solution is to engage with the most diverse range of people you can. Even sitting on your own, you can work on broadening your understanding.

STEP 1: Think of two related groups, one of which you belong to. It could be dog and cat owners, or it could your political party and one you oppose.

STEP 2: What do members of your in-group have in common? How do they differ?

STEP 3: What do members of the out-group have in common? How do they differ?

STEP 4: Did you see more diversity in your group than in the other? If so, go back and try to beef up your list of ways the out-group differs.

STEP 5: Find a common thread between both groups. For example, cat and dog owners both want to share their life with an animal.

☐ If you've thought of an out-group in a more personal and individual way, think of yourself as a winner.

WHY? WHY? WHY? WHY? WHY?

Nineteenth-century inventor Sakichi Toyoda had a simple system for getting to the root cause of problems: Ask "Why?" five times. It would be one of the key techniques that Toyota, the company he founded, would eventually use to become a global automotive giant.

It's a useful technique in everyday life, too. Why don't I like making lemonade? Because I don't like squeezing lemons.

Why? Because I find it painful.

Why? Because I have a paper cut on my finger.

Why? Because I used that finger to open an envelope.

Why? Because I don't have a letter opener.

Conclusion: The first step in making lemonade is "Buy a letter opener."

Sometimes you need only one "Why?" to get to the root cause. Sometimes you need dozens. View five as a guideline to make sure you don't stop too soon, rather than a mandate.

STEP 1: Ask yourself why you have a particular problem.

STEP 2: Ask "Why?" four more times (or until you've reached a root cause.)

STEP 3: Look back at your answer to each of those *whys*. Could some of the *whys* have alternative answers? You may find there are *multiple* root causes, all leading up to the effect you noticed.

☐ If you've kept asking "Why?" until you reached a root cause, why not give yourself the win?

THERE'S AN 85% CHANCE THIS TIP WILL MAKE YOU SMARTER

Experts love to throw probabilities at you. Your medicine has a 1 percent chance of side effects. Your lifetime risk of dying from a heart attack is 20 percent.

But what do those numbers *mean*? If the meteorologist says there's a 90 percent chance of sun and then it rains, were they wrong?

No! Weather forecasts aren't really about today—they're about days *like* today. "A 90 percent chance of sun" means that out of a hundred days like today, ninety will be sunny. That leaves ten days where you could get drenched.[1]

It's human nature to treat "unlikely" as "impossible." In fact, it's a common enough fallacy that it has its own name: **appeal to probability**.

STEP 1: Consider any probability that affects your life, from the weather forecast to your odds of winning the lottery.

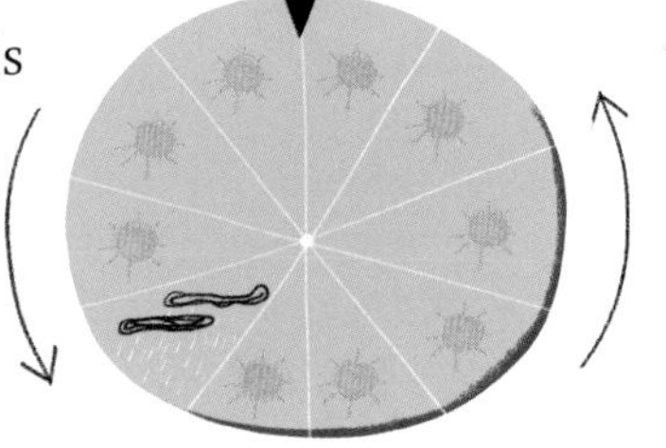

STEP 2: Drop the percentage symbol to convert that into "times out of a hundred."

STEP 3: Accept that probability is never a guarantee.

☐ If you've thought of one probability in terms of "times out of a hundred," give yourself 100 percent of the win.

1 There are two main schools of thought on probability. **Frequentists** ask, "How often does something happen?" **Bayesians** ask, "How confident am I that something happens in any one case?" I believe that the Frequentist approach is the clearest way to introduce people to statistics. If you are a Bayesian weather forecaster, you might feel I am oversimplifying your profession. I apologize. Please don't chase after me on a storm cloud, hurling bolts of lightning! (Okay, now I'm *really* misrepresenting your profession.)

DISTRUST SMALL SAMPLES

The last tip was about applying probabilities to real life. What about going the other way? How can you apply real life to probability?

There's a lot of complex math involved that's beyond the scope of this book to teach you. But one of the most crucial concepts is the idea of **sample size**. Consider the following kingdom.

If you counted the swans only in Lake 1, you'd conclude that swans have a 75 percent chance of being black. Meanwhile, at the other end of the kingdom, Lake 4-ites think it's more like 50 percent. By taking a small sample of the total swans, you risk getting an inaccurate answer.

In our mythical kingdom, there are only sixteen swans, and it wouldn't be too hard to count them all. But on earth, there are 7.8 billion people, and any entire life is only a small sample of human experience.

So next time somebody tells you, "I don't wear a seat belt, and I'm alive," point out that a sample size of one does not a study make.

STEP 1: Think about generalities you believe in—things you think are true about most people or that usually happen under specific circumstances.

STEP 2: Ask yourself how large a sample size you base that on.

STEP 3: Compare your sample size with the total population of stuff you're thinking about. If you were there 95 percent of the times your teeny pug encountered a bigger dog, you can be very confident about his probability of trying to attack a Bernese mountain dog. You should be less confident that every pug in the world behaves that way and less confident still that all living things do.

☐ If you've modified your confidence in proportion to your sample size, give yourself a proportionally big victory.

IF YOU HAD READ THIS FIRST, YOU COULD HAVE GOTTEN THIS BOOK CHEAPER

Whether it's with our boss or our six-year-old, we all find ourselves in occasional negotiations.

Good negotiators don't have to be hard-driving jerks. They just have to do their homework. Here are some tips from Harvard Law School's Program on Negotiation.

To learn more, read *Bargaining for Advantage: Negotiation Strategies for Reasonable People* by G. Richard Shell.

STEP 1: Set a specific and challenging goal for yourself, like "I'll negotiate a 10 percent higher fee than last time." It will likely lead to a better outcome than an unambitious or vague one.

STEP 2: Think about the question you least want the other side to ask. ("Has this car ever broken down?") Be prepared to answer it.

STEP 3: Figure out your own BATNA and your opponent's. **BATNA** stands for **B**est **A**lternative **t**o **N**egotiated **A**greement. Simply put, it's your backup option if negotiations break down.

STEP 4: See if you can find a way to improve your BATNA. Can you find a backup buyer in case this one tries to lowball you?

STEP 5: Look for concessions you can give that will be worth more to them than to you. If you're selling your entire cheese collection, you won't need your custom cheese freezer. Can you throw it in as a bonus?

STEP 6: Everything so far has been your preparation. Now it's time to actually start. There may be an advantage to making the first offer. That's thanks to a psychological phenomenon called *anchoring*, in which the first number we hear exerts a hard-to-resist pull over our thinking. (Remember, though: An opening price that's too far above the other side's BATNA may not be taken seriously.)

STEP 7: Negotiations don't have to be unfriendly. Asking your counterpart for their opinions can help find common ground and establish mutual respect. Maybe they have suggestions for a cheese-transportation service you can use to send them the goods.

STEP 8: Don't be afraid of silence. At best, your silence may prompt the other side to negotiate against themselves. At worst, it will give you time to absorb what's just been said.

STEP 9: Make concessions and offer rewards in stages, but deliver bad news all at once. That way, you let the other side feel as if they're getting multiple wins and fewer losses.

☐ If you've used negotiation techniques to get yourself a better outcome, give yourself the win.

Acknowledgments

A lot of people who are smarter than me helped me put this book together. In 2019, my agent, Joan Paquette, recognized that I'd click with the brilliant and passionate staff of Odd Dot and suggested I stop by their offices and meet them. That meeting has led to three books so far. Thank you, Joan, for that and for your ongoing insight, support, and cheerleading.

And speaking of Odd Dot's brilliant and passionate staff, thank you to Daniel Nayeri, Nathalie Le Du, Tim Hall, Christina Quintero, Kate Avino, Jen Healey, Barbara Cho, Kathy Wielgosz, and Tracy Koontz. I'm especially grateful to my editor, Justin Krasner, for bringing me on to this project and pushing me to make it the best it could be.

Thank you to Kevin T. Jones, PhD, at the Neurology Department at the University of California, San Francisco, who reviewed this manuscript and helped me understand the science. If I got things wrong despite his patience and care, that is entirely my fault

A special thank you to my wife, Lauren, and my children, Erin and Joe, for their patience over the many weekends and evenings I spent on the short-term crunch (page 106) of writing this book.